남겨진 민족
아랍의 기원과 연구과제

Research tasks on
the Origins of the Remaining Arab Peoples

남겨진 민족 아랍의 기원과 연구과제

2024년 10월 17일 초판 1쇄 발행

지은이 조다윗

도서출판 비전출판사
주소 서울특별시 서대문구 가재울로2안길 33 (03693)
전화 02-6414-7864
이메일 visionpd2@hanmail.net
홈페이지 www.wmuv.net
등록번호 제 312-2013-000011호

ISBN 979-11-87120-16-2 (93230)

ⓒ 조다윗 2024

Research tasks *on*
the Origins *of* the Remaining Arab Peoples

by David Cho

Copyright © 2024, by David Cho

이 책의 저작권은 저자와 도서출판 비전출판사가 소유합니다.
신저작권법에 의하여 한국 내에서 보호를 받는 저작물이므로
무단전재와 복제를 금합니다.

Research tasks *on* the Origins *of* the Remaining Arab Peoples
*Copyright 2024. Missionary David Cho and Vision Publishing House
all rights reserved.*

남겨진 민족
아랍의 기원과 연구과제

조다윗 선교사 지음

David Cho

Research tasks on
the Origins of the Remaining Arab Peoples

비전선교단

차례

머리말   9

감사의 말   11

**남겨진 민족 아랍의 기원과
이슬람 이전 아랍 고대사 연구과제**
- 아랍 부족주의를 중심으로

1. **아랍의 기원에 관한 문제제기**   13
   - 아랍 부족주의의 근원을 생각해보며

2. **아랍, 중동, 이슬람 역사 권위자들의**   15
   7세기 이슬람 이전 아랍 기원, 초기 역사 접근, 기술, 관점

3. **연구 제약을 넘어**   37
   - 아랍 유목문화 기록 부재와 헬라 지성에 수혈 받은
     이슬람 지적 아카이브 활용

4. **성경에서 본 아랍의 기원**   39
   - 이스마엘과 무함마드로 이어지는 아랍인 계보

5. **아랍의 기원 연구와 아랍학, 중동학, 이슬람학 개론 상**   41
   연구 범주 재정립
   - 북아프리카권, 중앙아시아권, 동남아시아권까지

6. **이슬람 이전 아랍 근간, 아랍 부족주의에 대한**   45
   이해 관점 현대 적용 사례
   - 이스라엘 하마스 전쟁과 평화 해법

참고도서   49

Contents

Preface 53

Thanks to 55

Research tasks on the Origins of
the Remaining Arab Peoples &
Pre-Islamic Ancient Arab History
- Focusing of Arab Tribalism

1. **Questioning the Origin of the Arabs** 57
   - Considering the Roots of Arab Tribalism

2. **Approaches, methodologies, and perspectives of** 60
   the origins of Arab and early history of pre-Islamic Arabs
   in the 7th century from Arab, Middle Eastern, and
   Islamic history authoritative scholars

3. **Beyond the Limitations of Research** - The Absence of ... 87
   Records on Arab Nomadic Culture and the Utilization of
   Islamic Intellectual Archives Influenced by Hellenistic
   Thought

4. **The Origins of Arabs in the Bible** - The Genealogy of Arabs ... 89
   Traced through Ishmael and Muhammad

5. **Research on Arab origins and Reevaluation of the Study** ... 93
   Scope in Introductory of Arab Studies, Middle Eastern
   Studies, and Islamic Studies - Including North Africa region,
   Central Asia region, and Southeast Asia region

6. **Understanding the Foundations of Pre-Islamic Arab** ... 97
   Society and Arab Tribalism: Modern Application Cases
   - The Israel-Hamas War and Peace Solutions

Reference 102

일러두기

이 글은 『선교타임즈』 2024년 7월호에 실린 초록을 개정·첨부 『이스라엘 하마스 전쟁으로 본 중동 극단주의 흐름』에 붙인 중동 소요 사태의 연구를 제외하고, 아랍의 기원과 역사 패러다임을 몸글 중심으로 개정증보 되었음을 밝힙니다.

머리말

 남겨진 민족 아랍족을 복음으로 섬기려 연구하는 가운데 7세기 이전에 아랍족의 역사가 대체로 간과되고 생략된다는 점이, 기이했다. 이슬람학, 중동학, 아랍학을 막론하고 이러한 이슬람 이전 아랍족 고유 역사에 대한 생략이나 약술의 관점이 대체로 거의 동일한 경향을 지닌다.

 BC2000년경 활동한 아브라함의 서장자 이스마엘로 시작된 아랍인의 기원을 처음으로, 아랍 쿠라이쉬족 일원 무함마드가 창시한 이슬람의 시작된, AD 7세기 경에 이르기까지, 약 2700년간의 고대 역사가 연대기조차 거의 빈약한 채로 어떻게 대개 역사가 약술, 간과될 수 있었을까.

 이 연구와 저술은 남겨졌으나 잃어버린 이러한 민족과 역사, 이스마엘의 후손 아랍족을 주님께로 돌리기 위한 관심과 이해, 사랑의 분투다.

 성경 전반, 혈육의 아버지가 아닌 하나님께로 직접 이름을 지어 받은 인물이 희소하고 드물다. 이스마엘은 하나님께서 직접 이름을 지어 부르셨다. 하나님께서 친히 아버지가 되어 아들 예수님의 복음을 보내 잃어버린 민족, 아랍을 구원하실 것이다.

2024년 10월 조다윗 선교사

감사의 말

책이 나오기까지 많은 영감에 자양분이 되어 준 믿음의 선진들과 더불어, 교정과 편집 작업을 도와준 유경은 간사, 박혜지 간사, 임아란 간사 고상한 북디자인을 해 준 권혁기 간사, 영문 번역을 맡아준 박시원 간사, 박은총 간사, 김희명 간사, 비전 선교공동체와 함께하는 350여명의 선교 사역자들 모두 감사하다.

말씀과 함께 살기 위해 공동체의 삶을 마다않고 더불어 함께 하는 아내와 은빛, 시후, 안녕이를 비롯한 가족들은 내 보석들이다. 우리가 아니더라도 누군가를 통해 주님이 어두운 시대를 밝힐 말씀의 횃불을 드실 것이나 말씀이 우리와 함께 하심에, 그래서 감사하다.

1. 아랍의 기원에 관한 문제제기
– 아랍 부족주의의 근원을 생각해보며

중동학, 이슬람학, 아랍학에는 이상하리만치 아랍에 관한 기원이 간과되거나 7세기 이전 역사가 미진하게 다루어진다. 이슬람을 열어 중동·북아프리카·중앙아시아·동남아시아 등지에 거대한 영향을 미친 아랍족은 희한하게도 내외부의 역사가들로부터 아랍 민족 기원과 근원에 대해 간과된 채로, 7세기 이후에 이슬람 종교의 체계화로부터 역사서술이 본격화되는 경우가 대부분의 아랍을 다루는 역사서술 방식이다. 아랍 민족은 7세기 이후에 갑자기 등장하여 이슬람 종교를 체계화하여 따르고 전파한 민족인가? 아랍 민족은 7세기 이전부터 존재해왔다. 그런데도 왜 아랍을 기원으로 한 이슬람, 중동 연구 역사에서 아랍민족의 근원이 간과된 측면이 강할까?

아랍사를 다루는 관점에서 있어 무함마드를 비롯한 이

븐 할둔(Ibn Khaldun)[1] 등 아랍 내부자로서 아랍 역사에 막대한 영향을 끼치거나 역사관점을 정립한 권위자들이 있다. 일단 이슬람을 창시한 무함마드는 아랍 역사에 있어 막강한 영향을 끼친 것이 주지의 사실이다. 그러나 그는 이슬람 이전의 아랍을 자힐리야(Jahiliya)[2]라는 무지몽매의 시대로 규정함으로써 이슬람 발생 이전의 아랍 시대를 홀대했고, 이븐 할둔 등 이슬람 아랍 중동 내부자적 관점으로 역사를 다루는 역사가들에게도 지대한 영향을 미쳤다. 결국 아랍 민족의 역사는 이슬람이 발호한 7세기 이후의 역사서술로 흡수, 초기 서두가 간략 개괄되게 되었다.[3]

---

[1] 14세기 튀니스 출신의 이슬람 역사가, 사상가, 정치가. 당시 혼란했던 북아프리카의 정치, 사회에 대해 최초의 사회학적 견해를 가지고 정리했으며, 당시 전통적인 이슬람 역사관과 차별되는 객관적, 비판적인 분석을 통해 역사의 본질과 역사 변천 과정, 인류 역사 흐름의 일반 법칙을 조명하려 시도했다. 주요저서로는 무캇디마(Muqaddimah, 역사서설, 이슬람사상, 1377) 등이 있다.
송경근, 「이븐 칼둔의 아사비야에 대한 연구」, 『한국중동학회논총』 제 36권 제 3호, 2016, p.69~92.

[2] '무지'를 뜻하는 아랍어에서 유래. 이슬람이 등장하기 이전 시대, 상태.

[3] "과거 자힐리야의 삶과 무슬림이 된 이후의 삶 사이에는 명확한 단절이 있어야 한다. 자힐리야와의 관계를 완전히 끊어냈을 때 무슬림은 비로소 완전히 이슬람의 품 안에 들어가는 것이다.", 사이드 꾸틉, 서정민 역, 『진리를 향한 이정표(이슬람 원리주의 혁명의 실천적 지침서)』, 평사리, 2011, p.73.

또한 버나드 루이스(Bernard Lewis), 한스 큉(Hans Kung) 등 서구에서 아랍 이슬람사를 바라본 학문적 권위자들의 경우도, 라틴을 이은 헬라족이 세운 비잔틴 제국으로 대표되는 서구와 7세기 이후 아랍이 이슬람으로 종교체제화 된 뒤에 조우한 아랍 이슬람이 서구가 본격적으로 경험한 아랍이기에, 7세기 이슬람 이전의 아랍에 대해 간과된 측면이 크다 하겠다.[4]

2. 아랍, 중동, 이슬람 역사 권위자들의 7세기 이슬람 이전 아랍 기원, 초기 역사 접근, 기술, 관점

앞서 언급한 이슬람 역사 기술의 권위자들은 이슬람 아랍 초기 역사에 대해 다음과 같은 연유로 간과, 간략 기술, 관점 부재 등의 양상을 지녀 아랍 역사 기원에 저변 패러다임과 관점 형성에 부재를 초래하였다.

---

4 전완경, 『아랍문화사』, 한국학술정보, 2013, p.42.

1) 무함마드와 자힐리야
-아랍 초기 기원 역사에 대한 결정적 부재 초래

 어떤 민족이나 나라가 스스로의 역사나 기원, 근원을 간과하기란 불가능에 가깝다. 스스로의 형성을 부정하는 일이기 때문이다. 그런데도 왜 아랍 역사 기술은 내부적으로 7세기 이전에 역사 형성이나 아라비아 기원에 대해 약술되거나 간과되는 측면이 커 보일까? 7세기 이후 아랍 사회에 이슬람이 형성되어 막강한 영향을 끼친 것은 주지의 사실이다. 그럼에도 불구하고 아랍 전체가 7세기에야 태동되고 나타난 민족이나 사회만이 아님에도, 아랍 관련 역사서술은 이슬람 이후의 역사로 본격 기술되는 경우가 대부분이고 그 이전 역사는 이슬람 태동기 전조로 간략 기술되거나 대체로 간과되어진다. 그 주된 원인은 아랍을 병합하여 이슬람을 창시한 무함마드가 이슬람 창시 이전에 역사에 관해 자힐리야라는 개념을 남겼고, 하이퍼 무함마드 퍼스널리티에 매몰되어있는 중동·아랍·이슬람·무슬림 사회에서 7세기 이전 아랍 사회 형성에 비중을 두기 어렵게 되었기 때문이다.

 이슬람 종교와 역사를 창시한 인물로 추앙받는 무함마드

자신의 이슬람 창시 이전 아랍과 아라비아 역사에 대한 인식은 쿠라이시족(Quraysh)을 제압하고 메카에 입성한 이후 그의 고별설교[5]에 잘 나타난다. 무함마드의 언행록 모범 하디스나 순나가 경전 쿠란과 더불어 이슬람교도들과 그 사회가 지키는 샤리야법 형성에 권위 준거가 된다. 더군다나 고별설교에 나타난 자힐리야라는 개념은 메디나에 이어 메카를 정복하고, 아라비아에 이슬람을 본격화한 직후 무함마드 생애 마지막 설교와 언행이라는 점에서 무슬림들에게 매우 중요한 가르침의 표본과 종교사회체계 전반에 준거로 인식된다.

무함마드는 메카를 정복한 뒤 기존 메카의 주 종족 쿠라이시 가문 등에게 화해의 제스처를 한뒤, 다음해 방문한 메카 카바와 아라파트 산 부근을 순행한 후 고별 설교에서 피의 복수를 벌이던 이전 시대정신을 '자힐리야', 무지의 정신이라 규정했다. 또 이제 이슬람과 무슬림 공동체가 메카를 흡수해 아라비아에 본격 출현한 이후, 이 자힐리야에서 벗어날

---

5   앨버트 후라니, 김정명 홍미정 역, 『아랍인의 역사』, 심산, 2010, p.181–182.

것을 선포했다.[6]

이러한 무함마드의 고별 설교의 권위를 따라 오늘날의 무슬림들과 아랍 역사가들은 이슬람 창시 이전에 아라비아와 아랍 상황을 자힐리야, 무지의 시대로 인식한다. 자힐리야의 무지라는 단어 본연의 개념은 본래 쉽게 화를 내는 성질, 명예와 위신에 대한 심각한 과민과 오만과 무절제, 또한 특히나 폭력과 보복에 대한 고질적인 경향을 뜻한다.[7]

따라서 이러한 자힐리야라는 개념은 아랍이 유일신 알라에 대한 관념을 보편적으로 받아들이기 전 부족 간의 반목과 할거, 그들의 오만한 자부심 등으로 인한 전쟁과 충돌을 다루고 있었다. 그러나 무함마드가 역설적으로 전쟁을 통해 메카를 정복한 뒤 갈등과 긴장, 전쟁을 주고받은 쿠라이시 부족등과 연대하기 위해 전쟁 이후 병합과 화평을 염두에 둔 표현으

---

6 "이 시기를 무슬림들은 "자힐리아", 즉 "무지의 시대라고 부른다. 물론 이 용어는 "여명의 시대"인 이슬람 시대에 대비된 개념이다. 이 시기는 그 이후에 새롭게 맞은 시기나 과거의 시기와 비교할 때 암흑의 시기였다. 이런 면에서 이슬람의 도래는 일종의 회복이라고 할 수 있고 꾸란에 명시된 대로 아브라함 종교의 회복이라고 할 수 있다.", 버나드 루이스, 『중동의 역사』, 까치(까치글방), 1998, p.49.
7 카렌 암스트롱, 김승완 역, 『무함마드 신의 예언자』, 교양인, 2024

로써 이전에 반목과 전쟁, 자힐리야에서 이제 벗어나야한다는 입장을 표명했고, 후에 무슬림들이 이에 권위를 두어 역사 해석의 기저로 삼게 된 셈이다.

하이퍼 무함마드 퍼스널리티에 매몰된 무슬림과 그 역사가, 종교지도자들은 모든 역사와 시대를 논할 때마다, 이슬람 이전에 아라비아 중동의 역사가 무지의 시대였음을 강조, 부각함으로써 이슬람 역사가 얼마나 찬란하며 영광스러운 것인가를 설파하는 관점, 기저를 지닐 수밖에 없다.[8]

예컨대 만약 어떤 아랍 내부 역사가가 이슬람 형성 전 아랍 남부 소문명에 대해 관심을 가져, 구전과 문헌 등을 통해 초기 문명 형성 요인, 언어, 문명적 요소와 그 발전 전개 양상을 기술한다고 하자. 무슬림 내부 역사가의 경우라면, 소문명의 태동·발전·전개·소멸과정 이후 아랍사회에 끼친 영향 등을 종합 기술해 갈 때, 자힐리야라는 개념은 학술적 권위를 넘어

---

8 "서남아시아와 북아프리카 그리고 주변의 광대한 지역, 후일 이슬람을 구성하게 된 지역, 칼리프의 통치권역, 오늘날 아랍 세계로 불리는 지역은 당시 서로 다른 언어를 사용하고 있었고, 다른 종교를 믿고 있었으며, 다른 통치자들에게 복속되어 있었다. 그런데 무함마드가 죽은지 거의 1세기 만에 그 지역 전체는 개조되었고, 인류 역사 상 가장 급격하고 가장 극적인 대변화를 맞이했다.", 버나드 루이스, 앞의 책, p.59.

서 교조적 권위로 작동하게 될 수 있다.

 이슬람 태동 이전에 아라비아는 무지의 시대라는 교조적 선포 아래 아라비아 남부 소문명도 아랍 사회 형성에 기여한 바 그 문명의 흥망성쇠 및 이후 아랍 사회의 반향 등을 기술해야한다면, 문명발전요소 진술은 이슬람 창시 전의 시대는 곧 어둠의 시대, 자힐리야라는 무함마드의 교조적 권위에 대한 반동 요소가 될 수밖에 없다.

 아라비아 남부 원시 소문명은 물론 쇠퇴기를 거쳤겠지만 문명적 체계를 띠어 아랍 형성 발전에 기여 요소도 분명히 존재했을 텐데 이러한 글을 기술하는 것은 곧 자힐리야라는 개념에 배치되는 측면이 있게 되는 것이다. (실제로 이슬람 이전 아랍 초기 문명의 기여 연구 요소는 무함마드가 자주 애용했던 구술 방식 중 하나인 아랍초기문명 전통 중 아랍 시(詩)에 대한 용인 정도로써 명맥이 이어지게 된다.)[9]

 따라서 연구자가 무슬림으로써, 이슬람 출현 이전 자힐리야 시대의 문명 기원 발전 가능성을 언급하고 상술하기란 이슬람 창시자 무함마드의 권위와 언행 중 특히 자힐리야 개

---

9 앨버트 후라니, 앞의 책, p.34-38

념에 배치되기에 아랍 초기 역사 연구와 기술에 큰 제약을 따르게 했다.

또한 자힐리야라는 무함마드의 고별설교 모티브는 현대 이슬람 극단주의 양상에도 큰 영감을 불어넣었다. 무슬림형제단의 2대 지도자이자, 현대 이슬람 극단주의 사상가인 사이드 쿠틉(Sayyid Qutb)은 샤리아법이 통치되지 않는 모든 역사와 영역을 자힐리야라 규정했다.[10] 서구 물질주의에 오염된 이슬람 체계나 역사 등을 무함마드가 형성한 진정한 초기 이슬람에서 벗어난 것으로 격하하면서 다른 사상으로 오염된 이슬람 왕조나 체계 역시 실질적 자힐리야에 있는 것으로 규정함으로써 배격과 척결을 주장하였다.

즉, 그의 주장에 따르면 샤리아가 적용되지 않는 모든 체제나 역사·시대성을 자힐리야의 회귀로 보고 무함마드의 언

---

10 "자힐리야가 이슬람 이전 시대에만 존재했던 것은 아니다. 오늘날 우리도 자힐리야에 둘러싸여 있다...우리를 둘러싼 모든 환경, 즉 사람들의 믿음과 사상, 습관과 예술, 규율과 법 등 모든 것이 자힐리야다. 심지어 우리가 이슬람 문화, 이슬람의 근원, 이슬람 철학 및 이슬람 사상이라고 간주하는 것들조차 자힐리야적 산물이라고 볼 수도 있다.초창기 무슬림들이 가르침을 받았던 그 순수한 근원, 즉 다른 것과 섞이거나 오염되지 않은 가장 순수한 근원으로 돌아가야만 한다.", 사이드 꾸틉, 앞의 책, p.74–75

행과 이슬람 창시의 광명에 반동으로서 배격 척결, 소멸시켜야 한다.

예컨대 이러한 쿠틉의 사상에 영향을 받은 극단주의자들에 의하면 현재 사우디아라비아가 이슬람국가임에도 미국에게 군사 기지를 제공한 점을 들어 서구체제를 돕는 악이고 어둠이며 자힐리야의 시대에 회귀로써 척결해야하는 역사나 체제가 된다.[11] 이처럼 형성된 역사성이나 체제까지 부정·소멸시킬 수 있는 자힐리야에 대한 현대의 극단적 해석은 곧 현대 이슬람 극단주의의 사상과 주요 모티브가 되어왔다.

2) 이븐 할둔의 아싸비야(al-asabiyyah)와 아랍부족, 아랍 초기사 기원 역사 기술 연관성

- 아싸비야 연대의식과 쿠라이시족
  무함마드 아싸비야를 통한 이슬람 체계 확립

---

11 "서구 기독교 세계가 주는 현재의 힘든 환경이 주는 압박과 지하드에 대한 사악한 오리엔탈리스트들의 공격이 있다", 사이드 꾸틉, 앞의 책, p.184
"극단주의 이슬람 성직자 오마르 압델 라흐만은 1990년 이집트에서 미국으로 건너가, 사이드 쿠틉의 '진리를 향한 이정표' 내용으로 설교했다. 그는 미국을 세계무슬림의 억압하는 나라로 규정하며 '신의 대적'에 맞서 싸우는 것이 의무라고 주장했다.", 9/11위원회, 「미국에 대한 테러 공격에 관한 국가 위원회의 최종 보고서(The 9/11 Commission Report)」, 2004, p.72

- 중세 이슬람 왕조 타락 가운데 대입 도출된
  아싸비야 역사관

  이븐 할둔은 이슬람 이전 아랍 초기 역사에 관련해 종교·정치 체계 이전 아랍 부족이나 전아 유목인 특성에 관해 분석한 학자로서, 또 아랍인 프로토타입에 관해 연구한 학자로서도 자리매김할 수 있겠다. 그러나 베두인족 등을 비롯한 아랍인 초기 유목인 형태에 대해 분석한 그의 연구는 이슬람 이전 아랍 기원이나 초기사를 연구하기 위한 목적이 아니었다는 점에서 초기 아랍사에 대한 그의 기여는 제한적이다.

  우선 이븐 할둔은 역사서설을 통해 아싸비야라는 부족 집단의 정신적 연대의식이 부족적 할거와 순수성을 결집시켜 정치·종교·문명체계를 이루는 역사관으로 동·서양 역사가들에게 막강한 영향을 끼쳤다. 또한 그러한 연대의식으로 출현한 왕조나 종교 문명 체제가 부족보다 강한 힘과 체계 결집을 갖다가 초기 순수한 연대 의식 정신을 잃어버린 왕조 체계 등의 사치, 치부, 윤리 도덕적 타락으로 체제 해체를 거치고 다른 아싸비야 집단의 도전을 통해 부족 왕조 종교 체제의 순환적 문명 흥망성쇠가 반복된다는 것이 그의 역사관에

요체다.[12]

이븐 할둔의 독특하고 특별한 역사의식과 그 학문적 기여는 중세 당대 전후의 역사가들의 기존 역사 철학 패러다임에 수혈 받은 영향이 없이 기술된 독보적 역사철학임을 아놀드 토인비(Arnold Joseph Toynbee)와 김호동 등은 말한다.

물론 역사서설은 이븐 할둔의 본인 철학 하에, 독자적인 구전 면담 자료, 도서관 서지 정보, 관료문서 수집 등을 통해 이루어진 세계사 기술을 위한 역사 서두일 뿐임에도, 아랍 부족, 도시인, 지식인, 문명, 왕조, 기후권 및 문명별 영향, 목축, 농경, 기술, 상업, 이윤, 축적 등에 방대한 개념과 관점을 망라한다는 점에서, 토인비조차 그의 업적을 인정한대로, 이슬람

---

[12] 역사서설에서 이븐 할둔은 다음과 같이 정리한다.
"아싸비야의 궁극적인 목표는 왕권이다 / 왕권의 장애물은 부족민이 사치와 안락함에 안주하는 것이다 / 왕권의 속성상 왕조는 영광을 독점하고 사치와 안정된 생활을 한 이후 노쇠기에 접어든다 / 왕조의 영역확대는 처음에 극에 달하고 그 뒤 차츰 줄어들어 마침내 왕조는 종말을 고하고 사라진다.". 이븐 할둔, 김정아역, 『무깟디마(The Muqaddimah) 이슬람 역사와 문명에 대한 기록』, 소명출판, 2020, p.230-232, 277, 486.

권에서도 독보적인 역사가의 위치를 점한다.[13]

    그럼에도 아무리 천부적, 천재적인 역사가라 하더라도 역사관에 대한 패러다임이나 관점의 수혈이 전혀 없이, 이슬람 왕조의 타락이 거듭되던 마그레브 아랍권 중세 시대에, 독자적으로만 이러한 역사서술을 성립했다고만은 볼 수 없겠다.

    이븐 할둔의 역사서설 속 아랍 부족과 아싸비야의 역사 인식에 영향을 준 패러다임을 재구성하기 위해, 그의 관점형성에 배경이 될 만한 상황과 관점을 먼저 이해할 필요가 있겠다. 먼저 이븐 할둔 당대에 중세 북아프리카 주변 아랍권 이슬람 왕조들이 타락한 상황 하에 마그레브에 아직 오늘날의 베두인 같은 왕조 체제와 도시 문명에 길들여지지 않은 베르베르, 베두인 아랍 부족 문화가 여전히 상존하고 있었다는 점이다. 두 번째 이븐 할둔은 어려서부터 꾸란을 암송할 만큼 이

---

13 "이븐 할둔은 자신이 선택한 지적인 활동의 분야에서 어떠한 선배로부터 영감을 받지 않은 듯하며, 자신의 동료들 사이에서도 어깨를 같이 할 만한 인물을 찾지 못했고, 어떠한 후배들에게도 영감의 불꽃을 일으키지 못했다. 그렇지만 그는 세계사에 첨부한 『역사서설』 속에서 독자적인 역사철학을 생각하고 형상화했는데, 그것은 이제껏 어느 곳, 어느 때, 어느 누구에 의해서 논의된 것보다 가장 위대한 작업임에는 의심할 여지가 없다." (저자, 아놀드 토인비의 『역사의 연구』에서 인용). 김호동, 「문명 성쇠의 비밀을 밝혀낸 이슬람의 고전-이븐 할둔의 『역사서설(歷史序說)』」, 『동양의 고전을 읽는다1(역사 정치)』, 휴머니스트, 2006

슬람 신앙에 대해 조예와 충심이 깊어 무함마드와 이슬람 신앙에 순수성에 매료된 사람이라는 점이다.[14] 따라서 이븐 할둔에게 무함마드는 쿠라이시 부족에서 파생된 인물이나 연대의식 즉 아싸비야를 작동시켜 부족의 할거와 분열을 종교 정신성으로 결집시켜 이슬람을 창시한, 칼리프 제국 체계 전조를 형성한 첫 번째 모델일 수밖에 없겠다. 다만 이븐 할둔은 그의 투철한 신앙심 때문에 학문적 질료나 연구 대상으로서 무함마드를 다루거나 대할 수 없고, 교조적 권위와 모델로서의 무함마드를 무슬림 신앙적 기조 안에서 대할 수밖에 없는 학술적 연구 한계가 존재한다. 따라서 이븐 할둔에게 무함마드는 종교적 권위며 그의 역사는 곧 전인적 패러다임이면서도 학술적 대상으로 질료화하거나 기술하기에는 학술적 권위 패러다임을 넘어서는 막강한 추종적 권위이다.

사실상 이러한 유추로 보자면 이븐 할둔의 아싸비야 연대의식의 가장 이상적인 모델은 이슬람을 창시한 무함마드이다. 쿠라이시 부족으로부터 난 무함마드는 알라로부터 계

---

14 "그(이븐 할둔)의 『자서전』에는 이 무렵 그가 이슬람의 경전인 『코란』과 예언자 무함마드의 언행을 기록한 『하디스』를 읽고 암송하면서, 아랍어 문법, 종교법, 신비주의 등에 관한 교육도 받았다고 기록되어 있다.", 김호동, 앞의 책.

시를 부여받고 이슬람이라는 종교를 창시하는 과정에서 모집단인 쿠라이시 부족으로부터 연대를 거절당해 근거지를 옮겼다. 그러나 다시 아랍 부족들을 종교정신성으로 재편해 메카를 수복, 쿠라이시 부족을 종교적 강한 연대의식으로 결합하고 재편한 인물이며, 곧 이는 부족을 연대의식 너머 체계, 이슬람 종교의 칼리프 정치체계를 낳았다.[15]

이렇게 이븐 할둔의 연대의식을 그의 종교성[16]과 중세 당대를 바라보는 역사가로서 재구성해보면 무함마드에게서 이상향으로 얻은 연대의식의 중세 마그레브 이슬람왕조, 즉 이

---

15 "종교는 그들의 오만함을 없애주고 그들이 서로 질투와 시기를 억제하도록 한다. 그들 중 예언자나 성자가 나타나서 알라의 명령을 이행하라고 명하고, 비난 받을 만한 기질들을 일소하고 칭찬받을 만한 덕성을 발달시켜 그들의 힘을 하나로 결집시키고 진리에 도달하도록 하면, 그들은 통합의 바탕 위에 지배력과 왕권을 획득 하게 된다. 그들은 올바른 인도 아래 종교적 진리를 수용하는 일에는 가장 빠른 속도를 보인다. 그 이유는 그들의 천성이 타락한 습관이나 비열한 자질에 감염되지 않았기 때문이다. 그들에게 단점이 있다면 '야만성' 인데 이것 역시 종교에 귀의하고 난 이후에는 쉽게 해결할 수 있는 문제 이다.", 이븐 할둔, 김정아 역. 앞의 책, p.250.

16 이븐 할둔은 아싸비야를 왕권에만 국한하지 않고 대표적으로 다음과 같은 경우에 기준이 되어 관여한다고 기술했다.
① 아싸비야는 아랍 베두인 부족에게만 존재하는 것이 아니다.
② 아싸비야는 포교 시에 절대적으로 필요하다.
③ 아싸비야는 꾸라이시 혈통이 이맘의 조건이라는 주장의 궁극적인 해답이다.
김정아. 「이븐 칼둔의 『무깟디마』에 나타난 아싸비야 (al-asabiyyah) 연구」, 『중동문제연구』 Vol.16 No.4, 2017, p.35-58.

븐 할둔 생애 당대 상황에 대한 적용일 수 있다. 즉, 부족끼리의 연대의식이 무함마드의 경우처럼 종교적 통일성 등으로 고양되어 칼리프체제, 왕조 체제 등으로 결집되었으나 중세 이슬람 왕조들의 타락상처럼 경제적 축적, 사치 등을 통한 타락으로 연대의식을 상실하고, 여타 주변 다른 부족 등에서 고양된 연대의식으로 결국 다른 왕조로 체제가 대체되는 이슬람 역사에 대한 교훈과 고찰인 셈이다.

따라서 아랍 원형에 아랍부족을 이븐 할둔이 날카로운 눈으로 분석하고 있긴 하지만 이것이 아랍 초기사의 복원과 연결 지어지기는 어렵다. 왜냐하면 왕조의 결집과 지속성이 중동보다 강하지 않았던 북아프리카권에 베르베르 베두인족의 아랍 부족 유목민 형태가 중세까지도 상존했지만 이러한 부족 구조나 형태에 대한 중세 당대 분석일 뿐 아랍 부족 초기사를 추적하는 연구로 이어지지는 않았다. 이븐 할둔이 구전 구술, 도서관, 왕정 서류 등까지 자료화할 수 있는 연구가였음에도 아랍 부족에 대한 연구가 그 기원을 추적하여 아랍 초기사 복원으로 이어지지 못한 것은 그의 막강한 연구 업적에도 불구하고 역사 기술 패러다임으로는 꽤 큰 손해였다.

3) 버나드 루이스(Bernard Lewis)의
   이슬람 이전 아랍사에 대한 부재, 생략으로써
   중동 역사 진술 방식

버나드 루이스의 경우 서구권의 대표적 아랍 중동 이슬람 학자로서 그의 저술과 관점은 무려 한 세기 동안이나 세계의 중동과 이슬람 아랍을 보는 눈에 막대한 영향을 끼쳤다. 영국의 학자로서 서구 주류 역사학계가 가진, 아카드·바벨론·페르시아·이집트로 이어지는 문명의 수혈을 통해 헬라·로마·유럽 문명을 형성한 역사 기술 패러다임을 고스란히 적층받은 채로, 튀르키예, 페르시아, 이집트, 유대 등등 그는 중동 권역 전반에 걸쳐 해박한 이해와 연구 업적을 가지고 있다.

그럼에도 불구하고 그의 중동사 전개에 아랍 고대 연구는 다른 고대 중동 권역의 해박함에 비해 비교적 미진하다. 무려 『아랍의 역사』, 『중동의 역사』를 생애에 걸쳐 동시대에 편찬한 만큼 중동사에서 적지 않은 비중을 차지하는 아랍사에 대해 각론을 진술할 수 있을 정도의 연구 역량을 가졌다. 그럼에도 그의 『중동의 역사』를 보면 그는 전반에 중동 고대 세계 역사를 훑으면서도 아랍의 기원부터 이슬람 등장 전 아랍 고대사에 대해서는 단 몇 줄에 분량으로 소급 언급을 할 뿐이다.[17] 자, 중동에서 이슬람을 창시하여 막강한 영향을 미친 아랍족의 고대사는 고유의 역사 길이로도 아브라함 이스마엘부터 기원을 잡는다면 족히 고대 BC 2000 경부터 시작된 역사다. 아랍사에 관한 대부분의 편중 기술이 무함마드 출현 이후 이슬람사로 편입 정리되고 이는 대략 AD 700 이후이니 현재까지 고작 1400여년의 역사다. 이슬람 출현 이전 아랍족의 시조인 이스마엘의 당대 생애부터 이슬람 등장 전까지 아랍의 고대 역사 길이는 무려 2700여년의 역사다. 각 민족이나 나라 문명 고대사가 약술되는 경우도 많으나 중동을 형성한 각 고유의 민족이나 문명의 고대역사의 개론과 각론이 이렇게까지 축약·빈약한 역사 분야는 이집트, 투르크, 페르시아, 바벨론, 히브리, 헬라, 로마 등등을 통틀어 아랍족이 거의 유일하다. 사실상 아랍의 역사로 각론을 언급할 수 없을 만큼 중동사나 이슬람사의 전조로써, 아랍족의 기원과 이슬람 등장 전 아랍 고대의 자취는 학문적 고대범주 카테고리도 가지지 못할 채로 미미하게 약술되다가, 통합 진술될 뿐이다.

---

[17] 버나드 루이스. 앞의 책. p.48-49

버나드 루이스는 세계사의 개괄처럼 중동고대사를 개괄하면서 바벨론, 이집트, 그리스 등지를 훑어 서구와 중동을 연결하는 가교로서 기독교 문명 배태 이전 중동고대사를 나열한다. 세계고대사개괄과 중동고대사개괄이 큰 차이가 나지 않는 접근법이다. 그 뒤에 동로마 기독교 비잔틴 제국의 노쇠와 조로아스터 페르시아 제국의 충돌, 한계와 퇴조를 그리면서 이슬람 문명이 등장하기 위한 문명적 요소에 전조를 논한다. 이 때 두 문명 간 충돌과 퇴조 전 고대 아라비아의 흑암기를 두 페이지 정도 언급하는 것이 이슬람 등장 전 아랍고대사에 관한 거의 전부다. 그 아랍고대사 역시 자힐리야라는 무함마드의 개념, 무지의 시대로 아랍인의 목소리를 빌려 간단히 축약할 뿐이다.[18] 또한 이 모든 중동고대사가 자힐리야 이후 이슬람의 내부자 무슬림의 시각과 관점으로, '찬란한 영광의 이슬람' 체계가 등장하기 위한 전조로서 전술될 뿐이다.

버나드 루이스는 서구의 오랜 '근동'이라는 용어를 넘어

---

18 "6세기는 두 경쟁자 모두의 위축이나 약화로 마감되었다…일련의 변화는 아라비아 반도에 상당한 영향을 끼쳤다..아마 가장 중요한 반응은 그들이 그들의 종교, 즉 그때까지 지켜왔던 원시적인 우상숭배에 만족하지 못하고 보다 나은 이념을 추구하기 시작했다는 점일 것이다.", 버나드 루이스, 앞의 책, p.50-54

중동이라는 지정학적 개념을 줄곧 사용함으로써, 서구 중심으로 본 유럽에서 가까운 동쪽이라는 의미의 '근동'을 극복한 듯 보인다. 그렇지만 아랍족이 발생시킨 이슬람으로써 중동사의 전조와 본격을 진술하면서도 이슬람 등장 전 아랍 고대사는 논외 밖이며, 거의 고려되지 않는다. 또한 중동사의 대부분을 서구가 본격적으로 조우한 7세기 이후에 아랍, 이슬람체계로서의 중동사를 본격 진술해갈 뿐이다. 이러한 버나드 루이스의 관점과 시각은 역시 앨버트 후라니(Albert Hourani) 같은 아랍계 영국인 학자의 저술 『아랍인의 역사』 등에서도 이슬람 등장 전 아랍고대사를 거의 연구대상으로 삼지 않은 채로, 서구 비잔틴과 페르시아의 오랜 전쟁과 충돌로 노쇠한 문명 이후에 본격 등장한 '찬란한 아랍·이슬람'이라는 관점으로 비슷하게 답습되고 있다.[19]

---

[19] 앨버트 후라니, 앞의 책, p.25-34

4) 카톨릭 사제 출신이자, 학자인 한스 큉(Hans Kung)의 아랍족 기원 이스마엘 이슬람 연구
- 비교종교학 입장에서 이슬람학 연구의 기독 복음주의적 관점 부재

한스 큉은 카톨릭 사제출신이자 동시에 소르본느 대학의 박사로서 카톨릭 토양과 진보주의 학문 토양의 자양분을 토대로 학술적으로는 이슬람과의 대화·소통의 비교종교 연구가로 알려져 있다. 기독계통의 이슬람 연구가로는 독보적인 연구 개괄 집대성의 결과물을 낸 사람이며, 유대교와 기독교 쪽으로도 학자이며 카톨릭 사제 출신이라는 점에서 다른 역사가들보다 내부 이해에 유리한 위치를 점한다. 그는 유대교, 기독교, 이슬람 3부작이라고 해도 좋을 만한 각 유일신 종교의 개괄 연구서를 망라하여 집필, 편찬한 사람이다.

따라서 자유주의 학자들과 이슬람 학자들에게는 자주 인용될 만한 기독계통의 이슬람 연구가로 알려져 있다. 안타깝게도 카톨릭 출신이면서 자유주의적 시각과 관점을 가진 이들 중 한스 큉만큼 이슬람에 대해 체계적 연구를 집대성할

만한 복음주의적인 개신교 계통의 학자는 부재하다. 따라서 대외적으로 그의 집대성 결과가 기독계통에 이슬람 연구의 대표적 패러다임으로 자리매김하고 있는 실정이다.

그의 아랍 기원사연구는 아브라함이라는 공통 분모로써 유대교와 기독교, 이슬람교의 기원을 찾아간다. 따라서 이슬람교의 시조인 이스마엘을 비롯한 아랍의 형성에 대해 밝히면서도 새뮤얼 헌팅턴(Samuel Huntington) 류의 문명 충돌 관점을 비판하면서 대화와 소통에 이해를 모색함으로써 세 문명의 공통분모 자취를 아라비아반도에서 추적하는 경향을 가진다. 이슬람교에 유일신 사상이 수혈, 배태된 점에 대해 아라비아 반도 근방의 유대교와 기독교인들의 영향력이 지대했던 토양적 배경도 밝힌다.[20]

그러나 한스 큉의 견해는 유일신 사상, 아브라함을 조상으로 하는 세 종교의 공통분모를 도출하는 이슬람 이전의 아라비아 토양을 그려 낸다. 그러면서 종국에는 이슬람에도 구원이 존재할 수 있으며, WCC와 가톨릭 당국에 교회 밖에도

---

[20] 한스 큉, 『한스 큉의 이슬람』, 시와진실, 2012, p.124-125.

구원이 있을 수 있음을 인정하라는 자유주의 다원론에 입각한 구원관을 제시, 수용하라고 압박한다.[21]

그는 갈라디아서에 나오는 이중 알레고리, 하갈 자손 이스마엘이 율법 안에 있는 육체의 자녀이며 곧 약속 밖에 자녀라는 구절을 의식해 이스마엘 후손 아랍의 무슬림들이 하나님의 약속 밖에 있는 백성이라는 성서의 풍유가 있음을 인정하면서도, 이것은 성경의 전반에 의도라기보다 일각의 진술이나 해석일 뿐이라고 바울의 교리를 폄하한다.[22] 이렇게 신약 성경의 권위를 호도해서라도 그는 이슬람 안에도 하나님의 약속과 구원이 있을 수 있다는 결론을 도출하기 위해, 기독교와 이슬람의 아브라함 종교로써의 공통분모를 추출해

---

21 "내가 이 질문을 이처럼 분명하게 제기하는 것은, 특히 세계교회협의회의 이중적인 태도 때문이다… 또한 그분의 뜻을 행함으로써 그 기원에서부터 이미 유대인이나 그리스도인과 가장 공통점을 많이 가진 사람들, 즉 무슬림이다… 그리스도교의 관점에서 볼 때도 이슬람은 구원에 이르는 길이 될 수 있다는 것이다.", 한스 큉, 앞의 책, p.129-130.

22 "그런데 히브리 성서에서는 아브라함의 아들, 사막의 아들 이스마엘이 이사악과 비교할 때 철저히 무시되고 있는 것 아닌가? 신약성서도 마찬가지 아닌가? 바울로 사도가 갈라디아인들에게 보낸 편지에 나오는 사라-하갈 알레고리는 이스마엘에 대한 완전한 경멸 아닌가? 이런 문제 제기에 정면으로 반박할 수는 없다. 그러나 그것은 한 측면에 불과하다.", 한스 큉, 앞의 책, p.116.

가는 방식으로 학문적 진술을 능수능란하게 활용한다.[23]

    그러나 이러한 복음주의 개신교 입장에서 전혀 받아들일 수 없는, 이슬람에 대한 기원과 아브라함의 공통 종교로써의 구원 가능성을 진술하고 있는 한스 큉의 견해가 대외적으로는 이슬람에 대한 기독교의 주류 학문적 입장으로 자리매김하고 있는 경향이 있다. 한스 큉의 비교종교로써 이슬람 연구를 집대성한 업적과 아성 때문에, 개신교 선교학이나 복음주의적 입장에서 받아들일 수 없는 한스 큉의 자유주의적 해석이 학문 계통에서는 기독교의 주류 입장으로 호도될 수 있다. 안타깝게도 아브라함의 서장자 이스마엘 탄생을 통해 아랍의 기원이 형성되었음을 밝히면서도 아랍기원과 이슬람 이전 고대 역사 및 이슬람에 대한 연구가 복음주의적 기독교의 선교적 관점으로 정리·정립되었다면, 대 학문적 기독교의 주류 입장으로 한스 큉의 견해가 일방적으로 독주하지만은 않았을 것이다. 한스 큉 이상의 개신교 선교학자들과 이슬람,

---

23 "이렇듯 아브라함이 처음에는 세 종교의 "공통분모"처럼 보이더니, "각 종교의 전통적 관점에 따라" 다시 한 번 보니까 오히려 "세 종교를 서로 갈라놓는 모든 것의 화신"으로 보이니, 아브라함을 "오늘날 대화의 이상적인 출발점"으로 삼는 일은 불가능한 것인가?", 한스 큉, 앞의 책, p.117–119, 123.

아랍권 선교사들의 아랍에 대한 기원 및 역사에 대한 복음주의적 관점의 종합적이고 탁월한 집대성 연구가 긴요하다.

3. 연구 제약을 넘어
– 아랍 유목문화 기록 부재와 헬라 지성에 수혈 받은 이슬람 지적 아카이브 활용

이처럼 아랍 역사 관점의 패러다임을 형성한 권위자들의 시각에서 서양, 중동 내부를 막론하고 아랍의 근원에 대해 간과된 측면이 크다. 또한 아랍은 이슬람 종교 체계화 이전에 유목민으로 살아온바 정주(定住)적 기록 문화가 약했으며[24], 따라서 이슬람 체제 이전의 아랍에 대한 기록이 많지 않은 것도 아랍의 기원과 이슬람 이전의 역사에 대해 연구하기에 불리한 측면으로 작용한다. 그러나 이슬람은 구약과 신약의 내러티브를 차용해 간 꾸란의 내적 모순이 커, 성서의 내적 일관성과 통일성에 비견될 수 없는바, 이슬람 경전의 모순을 헬라

---

24 전완경, 앞의 책 p.18~20.
한스 큉, 앞의 책, p.80–84.

지성의 매개변증으로 메우려한 측면이 있다. 이것은 아이러니하게도 이슬람 사회에 헬라지성 수혈의 길을 열어 아랍 지중해권의 각종 도서관, 아카데미 건립 등을 통해 지적 축적을 가져오기도 했다.[25] 따라서 아랍의 비교적 정확한 구전 구술 문화와 이슬람 이후 헬라 조우를 통해, 아랍 사회에 체계적으로 남아 있는 지적 아카이브를 활용해 아랍의 기원과 개론, 이슬람 이전 역사에 관해 학문적 패러다임을 새로이 열 수 있는 현장 연구가(研究家), 이론가이자 동시에 선교사인 자원이 학문적 체계화에 도전해 보면 좋겠다. 아랍의 기원과 이슬람 이전에 역사 영역은 중동의 실체를 파악하는데 매우 긴요하면서도 강력한 통찰력을 제공할 터이나 앞서 말한 연유 때문에 학문적 연구 영역으로도 거의 손대지 않은 무주공산에 가깝다. 중동 아랍에 관해 막대한 학문적 연구가 고대 중세로부터 현대까지 이어져 왔으나, 이 영역은 개척의 연구 영역으로 남아 연구 성과가 입증된다면 학문적 패러다임과 새로운 틀을 열만한 분야일 것이다.

---

25 브리태니커 편찬위원회, 『브리태니커 필수 교양사전 이슬람』, 아고라, 2017, p.74~85.

4. 성경에서 본 아랍의 기원
– 이스마엘과 무함마드로 이어지는 아랍인 계보

의외롭게도 아랍인들은 사우디아라비아를 중심으로 한 남부 아랍인을 '카흐탄(Qahtan)'이라 명명하면서도 그들을 이스마엘과 무함마드를 잇는, 혈통적·영적 적통으로 말하지 않는다. 오히려 북부 아랍인들을 '아드난(Adnan)'이라 명명하면서 그들을 이스마엘과 무함마드를 이은 혈통적·영적 적통으로 말한다.[26] 구약을 통해 이스마엘이 아브라함 가계에서 쫓겨나 이집트 출신인 하갈이 이집트의 경계에서 길을 잃어 아라비아로 남하한 것은 자명하다.[27] 그런데 왜 북부 아랍인을 아랍인 스스로 이스마엘-무함마드를 이은 혈통적 직계라 생각하는 것일까? 일반적으로 아랍인들은 어느 가문, 누구의 아들로 이름이 표기될 정도로 혈연적 계통이 명확히 전승되어왔으며 결국 그 근원적 연유는 성경까지 올라가 아랍인의 조상, 이스마엘 가문과 에서의 결혼에서 답을 찾을 수 있다. 성경에서 보면 북부 아랍인의 정체와 근원이 나오는데

---

[26] 전완경, 앞의 책, p.22~25.
[27] 그가 바란 광야에 거주할 때에 그의 어머니가 그를 위하여 애굽 땅에서 아내를 얻어 주었더라(창 21:21)

아랍인의 시조 이스마엘의 딸이 에서와 결혼한 일이 기록되어 있다.(창25:13, 28:9)[28] 또한 북부에서 이스마엘의 차자, 게달 계통 등의 자손도 번성하여 아라비아와 함께 열거된다.(사60:6-7, 겔27:20-22)[29]

그리하여 북부 아랍인이 이 계통에서 형성되었는데 오늘날 요르단, 레바논, 시리아, 팔레스타인 등지에서 볼 수 있고, 이 북부 계통 아랍인 중에서 이슬람을 창시한 무함마드가 나왔다. 따라서 이스마엘-무함마드를 잇는 혈통적 계보는 사우디아라비아의 남부 아랍인에 근거하지 않고 북부 아랍인임을 오늘날에 아랍 사회도 인정하는 바다.

또한 아랍사회를 이해할 때, 이슬람체계가 막대한 영향

---

[28] 이스마엘의 아들들의 이름은 그 이름과 그 세대대로 이와 같으니라 이스마엘의 장자는 느바욧이요 그 다음은 게달과 앗브엘과 밉삼과(창25:13)
이에 에서가 이스마엘에게 가서 그 본처들 외에 아브라함의 아들 이스마엘의 딸이요 느바욧의 누이인 마할랏을 아내로 맞이하였더라(창28:9)

[29] 허다한 낙타, 미디안과 에바의 어린 낙타가 네 가운데에 가득할 것이며 스바 사람들은 다 금과 유향을 가지고 와서 여호와의 찬송을 전파할 것이며. 게달의 양 무리는 다 네게로 모일 것이요 느바욧의 숫양은 네게 공급되고 내 제단에 올라 기꺼이 받음이 되리니 내가 내 영광의 집을 영화롭게 하리라(사60:6-7)
드단은 네 상인이 되었음이여 말을 탈 때 까는 천을 너와 거래하였도다. 아라비아와 게달의 모든 고관은 네 손아래 상인이 되어 어린 양과 숫양과 염소들, 그것으로 너와 거래하였도다. 스바와 라아마의 상인들도 너의 상인들이 됨이여 각종 극상품 향 재료와 각종 보석과 황금으로 네 물품을 바꾸어 갔도다(겔27:20-22)

력으로 아랍 위에 적층되긴 하였어도 아랍 근간이 성서에 기록된 가족단위의 부족으로 나누어 할거·집산되어, 아랍을 형성한바 아랍 고유의 정신성이나 내적 질서를 이해할 때 더욱 먼저 아랍 근간 고대 아랍부족주의를 이해할 필요가 있다.

5. 아랍의 기원 연구와 아랍학, 중동학, 이슬람학 개론 상 연구 범주 재정립
 – 북아프리카권, 중앙아시아권, 동남아시아권까지

아랍의 기원이 성서에서 근거한 바, 이스마엘 느바욧의 딸 에서의 혼인과 이스마엘의 다른 아들들 게달 계통 등에 발달해, 통칭 북부 아랍인의 형성되어 무함마드 계보에 이르기까지, 혈통적 아랍에 계보와 이슬람을 연 창시자의 계열까지 연유를 찾을 수 있겠다. 이러한 아랍의 기원과 이슬람의 발생에 이르는 계통적 아랍을 구분하면 그간 아랍 이슬람의 영향을 받은 많은 지역의 학문적 연구개론 카테고리에 재정립 필요성을 생각하게 된다. 크게 아랍 이슬람에 영향을 받았던 지역 등은 물론 중동, 북아프리카, 중앙아시아, 동남아시아 등지 이다. 그럼에도 이들을 연구하는 학문 연구 범위와 그 구분을 나누는 기준은 아랍 혈통에 의한 것인지, 언어적 호환성에 따른 것인지, 이슬람 종교 정신성에 입각한 것인지, 지정학적 위치에 따른 것인지 모호했다.

중동이라는 개념은 근동이라는 서구 중심 지정학적 개념에 반발하여 나온 개념이다. 따라서 아랍과 이슬람이 발호한 핵심 지역임에도 중동학, 중동권이라는 말은 아랍 이슬람의 특성을 담기에는 불명확한 지정학적 개념일 뿐이다.[30]

우선 혈통적, 민족적 아랍은 전술했다시피 이스마엘과 무함마드에 이르는 계보의 직계를 중심으로 북부 아랍과 남부 아랍으로 나뉜다. 여기서 혈연적 직계는 북부 아랍이나 이슬람이 메카, 메디나를 중심으로 남부 아라비아에서 발호했다는 점과 여전히 이슬람 종교 구심력이 사우디아라비아에서 작동된다는 점에서 아랍의 7세기 이후 종교 정신성에 입각

---

[30] 인남식(국립외교원 교수), 2022.
https://www.youtube.com/watch?v=FHcm7B_VjVE

한 아랍의 핵심은 사우디아라비아의 남부 아랍이다.[31]

    그렇다면 북아프리카 아랍과 중앙아시아, 동남아시아 이슬람권 연구 범위를 나누는 기준은 과연 중동처럼 지정학적 개념으로 구분된 것인가? 아랍이라는 개념에 혈연적 민족적 단위로 구분한 것인가? 아니면 이슬람이라는 종교정신성을 기준으로 나눈 것인가? 기준이 모호하다. 북아프리카는 이슬람의 영향을 받아 북아프리카 '아랍'이라는 개념으로 두리뭉실하게 통술하면서도, 중앙아시아 역시 이슬람에 영향을 받은 지역임에도 중앙아시아 '아랍'이라는 말이나 학문적 연구 범위로 통술하거나 개념화하지 않는다. 그렇다면 북아프리카 권역이 이슬람의 영향을 받았다고 해서 혈통적, 민족적 아랍인가? 남부, 북부 아랍인처럼 혈통적 연관성이 북아프리카 민족에 거의 없는데도 북아프리카 '아랍'이라는 단어를 쓰는 이유는 무엇인가? 따져보면 사실상 북아프리카 '아랍'은 언어적 호환성으로 구분된 개념이다. 현재 북아프리카권은 이슬람화 된 뒤에 중앙아시아와 다르게 현재도 공시적 아

---

[31] 전완경, 앞의 책, p.33–34.

랍어를 사용, 통용하는 지역이다.[32] 그래서 북아프리카 '아랍'권의 '아랍'은 혈연적, 부족적, 민족적, 종교 정신적인 구분 개념이라기보다 아랍어라는 공시 언어 호환성에 따른 구분 기준인 셈이다.

한편 중앙아시아와 동남아시아는 이슬람의 영향으로 꾸란이 아랍어로 보급되어 문자 아랍어의 영향권 하에 있기도 하나, 북아프리카처럼 아랍어를 자신들의 통용 언어로까지 받아들이지는 않았다. 그래서 중앙아시아 '아랍', 동남아시아 '아랍'이라는 개념은 북아프리카 '아랍'처럼 통용되지 않는다.

결론적으로 중동, 아랍, 이슬람, 북아프리카아랍, 중앙아시아 동남아시아 이슬람 연구에는 좀 더 정밀하고 일관된 학문적 연구 범위와 범주 구분 기준이 필요하다. 이렇게 학문적 연구 범위가 지정학적 개념, 언어적 개념, 혈통적·민족적 개념, 종교적 개념이 뒤섞여 학문적 합의 기준이 없는 연구 분야도 드물다. 성서에서 비롯된 아랍의 기원에 관한 연구가 간과되거나 미진한 채로 7세기 이후 이슬람 발호와 서구와 조우하

---

[32] "모로코의 한 대학교수는 "아랍주의는 본질적으로 언어와 문화"라고 주장한다", 전완경, 앞의 책, p.36.

는 지정학적 영향 등으로만 기술되어 그렇다고 보여진다. 첫 단추가 애매모호하게 끼워진 셈이다.

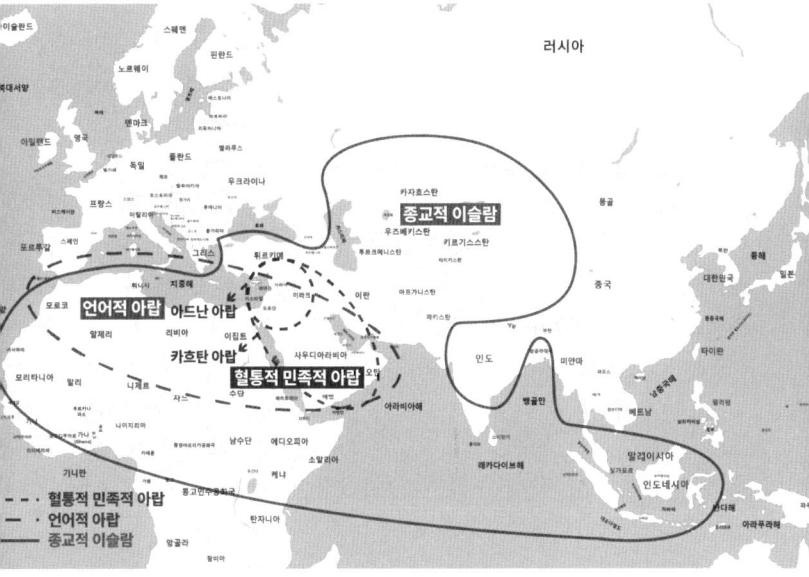

6. 이슬람 이전 아랍 근간, 아랍 부족주의에 대한 이해 관점 현대 적용 사례
– 이스라엘 하마스 전쟁과 평화 해법

최근에 서구권을 중심으로 이스라엘 하마스 전쟁을 바라보면서 연방론이 새롭게 제시되었다. 기존 국제사회의 해법으로 제시되었던 이스라엘 팔레스타인 두 국가 해법[33], 이스라엘 중심에 일 국가 일 체제론[34]이 대두되어왔으나 현실화되기 난망했으니 미국처럼 이스라엘과 팔레스타인의 각 자립을 인정하면서 느슨한 연방 국가를 구성하면 어떠하겠냐는 제의다. 일 국가론이 완전한 결혼이고, 두 개 국가론이 이

---

[33] Two-state solution, 유대민족을 위한 이스라엘과 팔레스타인 민족을 위한 팔레스타인을 설립함으로 이스라엘과 팔레스타인 분쟁을 해결하기 위한 제안으로 1993년 오슬로협정(Oslo Accords)의 일환이다.
브리태니커, https://www.britannica.com/topic/two-state-solution

[34] One state solution, 유세프 무나이어(예루살렘기금 팔레스타인 센터 사무총장)는 '팔레스타인 사람에게 동등한 권리를 보장하는 헌법을 제정하고 진상조사와 보상을 통해 과거사를 극복하고 단일 국가를 세우자'고 주장했다. 포린어페어스(Foreign Affairs), 2019.

혼이면, 연방 국가론[35]은 마치 합의 동거와 같다는 예시를 들며 국제사회에 호소된 견해이다. 그러나 이런 시각은 엄연히 서구체제의 모티브를 차용할 뿐 중동 일대와 아랍 사회의 근원과 특수성을 잘 모르고서 아전인수(我田引水)격으로 이 극한의 대립을 풀어보려는 시도이다.

왜냐하면 중동 아랍 이스라엘 갈등의 근원을 형성한 이스마엘과 이삭의 고대 갈등[36]은 사실은 중동에 부족주의의 원한과 원수맺음에 근거한 '눈에는 눈, 이에는 이' 고대 중동 율법과 그 유전이 대대로 중동 내부에서 흘러 내려 전하여져 오기 때문이다. 이는 이슬람이 체계화되기 전 중동 아랍의 뿌리에 근거한 유전이나 무함마드조차 이런 프로토타입(prototype)의 아랍의 부족주의를 극복하지 못했다. 무함마드는 유일신 사상으로 부족주의를 통합한 이슬람 이전에 부

---

35 서안 지구 7개 주요 부족들이 UAE식의 연방을 구성해 국제사회가 건국을 지원하는 케다르 플랜(여덟 국가 해법)도 있다, 인남식, 2018.

36 사라가 본즉 아브라함의 아들 애굽 여인 하갈의 아들이 이삭을 놀리는지라. 그가 아브라함에게 이르되 이 여종과 그 아들을 내쫓으라 이 종의 아들은 내 아들 이삭과 함께 기업을 얻지 못하리라 하므로(창 21:9–10)

족 갈등과 분열 사회 양상을 자힐리야라 했으나, 무함마드조차 아랍 부족주의의 원한관계로부터 자유로울 수 없었다. 메카에서 메디나로 이주 당시 선지자를 자처한 자신을 무시했던 아랍 유대인들을 원한관계로 보복, 무참히 학살하고 그 부녀자들을 노예 삼아 부리다가 그들의 원한으로 독살당한 것이 무함마드의 생애의 끝이었다.

따라서 '눈에는 눈, 이에는 이'에 중동 아랍의 율법 유전 전통은 오늘날에 아랍을 해석하는데 근간이 된다. 이스라엘 하마스 전쟁 간 이스라엘과 하마스, 팔레스타인, 아랍 이슬람 사회 간 극한 대립을 나이브하게 단순 서구렌즈로 투과해 체제 구조로 해석하는 것은 아랍의 뿌리를 간과해서이다. 아랍 부족주의의 은원관계는 체제나 정부, 종교보다 우선적이며 근원적이다. 따라서 이스라엘 하마스 간 전쟁은 부족주의에 입각한 원한을 짙게 할 뿐, 체제나 거버넌스 구조, 국제기구의 견제와 제안을 통해 해결될 수 없고, 오직 율법의 요구를 이기고 완성한 용서의 복음과 화해의 소식만으로 평화가 가능하다 하겠다.

참고도서

· 김정아, 「이븐 칼둔의 『무깟디마』에 나타난 아싸비야 (al-asabiyyah) 연구」, 『중동문제연구』 Vol.16 No.4, p.35-58, 2017.
· 김호동, 「문명 성쇠의 비밀을 밝혀낸 이슬람의 고전-이븐 할둔의 『역사서설(歷史序說)』」, 『동양의 고전을 읽는다1(역사·정치)』, 휴머니스트, 2006.
· 버나드 루이스, 『중동의 역사』, 까치(까치글방), 1998.
· 브리태니커 편찬위원회, 『브리태니커 필수 교양사전 이슬람』, 아고라, 2017.
· 사이드 꾸뚭, 서정민 역, 『진리를 향한 이정표(이슬람 원리주의 혁명의 실천적 지침서)』, 평사리, 2011.
· 송경근, 「이븐 칼둔의 아사비야에 대한 연구」, 『한국중동학회논총』 제36권 제3호, 2016.
· 앨버트 후라니, 김정명 홍미정 역, 『아랍인의 역사』, 심산, 2010.
· 이븐 할둔, 김정아 역, 『무깟디마(The Muqaddimah) 이슬람 역사와 문명에 대한 기록』, 소명출판, 2020.
· 이븐 할둔, 김호동역, 『역사서설 아랍, 이슬람, 문명』, 까치(까치글방), 2003.
· 전완경, 『아랍문화사』, 한국학술정보, 2013.
· 카렌 암스트롱, 김승완 역, 『무함마드 신의 예언자』, 교양인, 2024.
· 한스 큉, 『한스 큉의 이슬람』, 시와진실, 2012.
· 9/11위원회, 「미국에 대한 테러 공격에 관한 국가 위원회의 최종 보고서(The 9/11 Commission Report)」, 2004

차례

머리말 9

감사의 말 11

**남겨진 민족 아랍의 기원과
이슬람 이전 아랍 고대사 연구과제**
- 아랍 부족주의를 중심으로

1 **아랍의 기원에 관한 문제제기** 13
   - 아랍 부족주의의 근원을 생각해보며

2 **아랍, 중동, 이슬람 역사 권위자들의** 15
   7세기 이슬람 이전 아랍 기원, 초기 역사 접근, 기술, 관점

3 **연구 제약을 넘어** 37
   - 아랍 유목문화 기록 부재와 헬라 지성에 수혈 받은
     이슬람 지적 아카이브 활용

4 **성경에서 본 아랍의 기원** 39
   - 이스마엘과 무함마드로 이어지는 아랍인 계보

5 **아랍의 기원 연구와 아랍학, 중동학, 이슬람학 개론 상** 41
   연구 범주 재정립
   - 북아프리카권, 중앙아시아권, 동남아시아권까지

6 **이슬람 이전 아랍 근간, 아랍 부족주의에 대한** 45
   이해 관점 현대 적용 사례
   - 이스라엘 하마스 전쟁과 평화 해법

참고도서 48

Contents

	Preface	53
	Thanks to	55

Research tasks on the Origins of the Remaining Arab Peoples & Pre-Islamic Ancient Arab History
- Focusing of Arab Tribalism

1. **Questioning the Origin of the Arabs** — 57
   - Considering the Roots of Arab Tribalism

2. **Approaches, methodologies, and perspectives of the origins of Arab and early history of pre-Islamic Arabs in the 7th century from Arab, Middle Eastern, and Islamic history authoritative scholars** — 60

3. **Beyond the Limitations of Research** - The Absence of Records on Arab Nomadic Culture and the Utilization of Islamic Intellectual Archives Influenced by Hellenistic Thought — 87

4. **The Origins of Arabs in the Bible** - The Genealogy of Arabs Traced through Ishmael and Muhammad — 89

5. **Research on Arab origins and Reevaluation of the Study Scope in Introductory of Arab Studies, Middle Eastern Studies, and Islamic Studies** - Including North Africa region, Central Asia region, and Southeast Asia region — 93

6. **Understanding the Foundations of Pre-Islamic Arab Society and Arab Tribalism: Modern Application Cases** - The Israel-Hamas War and Peace Solutions — 97

Reference — 102

Notice

This article is a revised and expanded version of the abstract
published in the July 2024 issue of 『Mission Times』,
titled "A Study on the trends and flows of Islamic extremism in
the Middel East viewed from the Israel–Hamas war"
It clarifies that, except for the research on
Middle Eastern conflicts, the origins and historical paradigms
of the Arab world have been revised and expanded,
with a focus on the main text.

Preface

As I was studying to serve the remaining Arab people, with the Gospel, I found it strange that the history of the Arab people before the 7th century is largely overlooked and omitted. Whether in Islamic studies, Middle Eastern studies, or Arab studies, there is a similar tendency to either omit or briefly summarize the unique history of the Arab people before Islam.

Starting with the origins of the Arab people from Ishmael, the firstborn son of Abraham, who lived around 2000 BC, to the rise of Islam founded by Muhammad, a member of the Quraysh tribe, around the 7th century AD, how could approximately 2,700 years of ancient history have remained so sparsely chronicled and largely overlooked?

This research and writing are a struggle of care, understanding, and love to bring back to the Lord this people and history—descendants of Ishmael, the Arab people, who have been remained yet lost.

Throughout the Bible, it is rare for a person to be given a name directly by God rather than by their earthly father. Ishmael was one such person, named by God Himself. God will personally be a Father and send the Gospel of His Son Jesus to save the lost people—the Arabs.

Oct. 2024. Missionary David Cho

Thanks to

Thanks for all advanced of faith who was being inspiration of nourish- ment and also I thank you all staff Kyoungeun Yu, Hyeji Park, Aran Lim who helped proofreading and editing, and staff Hyeog-gi Gwon who did graceful design, and staff Siwon Park, Eunchong Park, Hee Myeong Kim who did translation, and about 350 mission staffs who works together in Vision Mission community.

My family a wife and Eunbit, Sihoo and Annyeong are my treasures who never reject the community lifestyle to live with the word of God. Of course the Lord will pick up the torch of His word to light dark age beside us, but that is why I am really appreciate His word is with us.

Notice

This article was written around January 2024.

I would like to inform you that the introduction has started to be written in the form of a column for the column contribution to 『Korean Journal of Frontier Missions』.

1. Questioning the Origin of the Arabs
- Considering the Roots of Arab Tribalism

In Middle Eastern, Islamic, and Arab studies, the origin of the Arabs is strangely overlooked, and the history before the 7th century is insufficiently addressed. The Arab people, who greatly influenced regions such as the Middle East, North Africa, Central Asia, and Southeast Asia through the rise of Islam, have had their origins and roots largely neglected by internal and external historians. Most historical narratives that deal with the Arabs tend to focus on the 7th century onward, beginning with the formalization of the Islamic religion. Are the Arab people a nation that suddenly emerged after the 7th century to systematize, follow, and spread Islam? The Arab people existed well before the 7th century. So why, in the study of Islam and Middle Eastern history, is the origin of the Arab people so frequently overlooked?

From the perspective of writing Arab history, there are figures such as Muhammad, Ibn Khaldun[1], and others who, as internal members of the Arab community, greatly influenced the historical narrative or established authoritative perspectives on Arab history. It is a well-known fact that Muhammad, the founder of Islam, had an enormous impact on Arab history. However, by defining the pre-Islamic Arab period as an era of ignorance and foolishness known as Jahiliya[2], he effectively down-played the significance of the Arab era before the rise of Islam. This profoundly influenced historians who approached history from an Islamic, Arab, or Middle Eastern internal perspective, including figures like Ibn Khaldun. As a result, the his-

---

[1] A 14th-century Tunisian Islamic historian, thinker, and statesman, he systematized the first sociological insights into the turbulent politics and society of North Africa at the time. Through his objective and critical analysis, which differed from the traditional Islamic historiography of the time, he attempted to shed light on the nature of history, the process of historical change, and the general laws of the flow of human history. His major works include the Muqaddimah(An Introduction to History, History of Islamic Thought, 1377).
Song Kyung-Keun, 「A Study on the Asabiyah of Ibn Khaldun」, 『Collection of writings of Korean Association Of The Middle East Studies』 Book No.36, Ch.3, p.69-92, 2016.

[2] Derived from the Arabic word for 'ignorance.' A state of affairs that existed before the emergence of Islam.

tory of the Arab people became subsumed under the broader history of Islam after the 7th century, with the earlier period often being reduced to a brief summary.[3]

Also, in the case of academic authorities in the West who have studied Arab Islamic history, such as Bernard Lewis and Hans Küng, it can be said that there has been a significant oversight regarding pre-Islamic Arabs before the 7th century. This is because the Arabs that the West primarily encountered were the Arab-Islamic civilization, which had become a religious system following the 7th century, and this encounter took place largely through the Byzantine Empire, established by the Hellenistic peoples succeeding the Romans.[4]

---

3 "There must be a clear break between the life of Jahiliya and the life of a Muslim. Only when the relationship with Jahiliya is completely severed can a Muslim truly enter the embrace of Islam.", Sayyid Qutb, Translated by Jung Min Seo, 『Milestones』, Pyung Sa Li, 2011, p.73.

4 Jeon Wan Gyung, 『Arab Cultural History』, Korean Studies Information, 2013, p.42.

2. Approaches, methodologies, and perspectives of the origins of Arab and early history of pre-Islamic Arabs in the 7th century from Arab, Middle Eastern, and Islamic history authoritative scholars

The aforementioned authoritative scholars of Islamic history exhibited tendencies such as oversight, brief descriptions, and lack of perspective regarding the early history of Islamic Arabs for the following reasons, leading to an absence in the formation of foundational paradigms and perspectives on the origins of Arab history.

1) Muhammad and Jahiliya-Resulting in a critical lack of early Arab origin history

It is nearly impossible for any nation or people to overlook their own history, origins, or roots, as doing so would be akin to denying their own formation. Despite this, why does the recording of Arab history seem to largely overlook or briefly summarize the formation of history and the origins of Arabia before the 7th century? It is well-known that Islam took shape in Arab society after the 7th century and exerted a powerful influence. Nevertheless, even though the Arab people and society existed long before the 7th century, most historical accounts regarding Arabs are written primarily from the period following the emergence of Islam, while the history prior to that is often briefly mentioned as a precursor to the rise of Islam or largely overlooked. The main reason for this is that Muhammad, who unified the Arabs and founded Islam, left the concept of Jahiliya to describe the pre-Islamic era. In Middle Eastern, Arab, Islamic, and Muslim societies, which are deeply immersed in the hyper-personality of Muhammad, it has become difficult to place significant emphasis on the formation of Arab society before the 7th century.

Muhammad's understanding of pre-Islamic Arab and Arabian history, as the figure revered for founding Islam as a religion and a historical movement, is well reflected in his Farewell Sermon after he subdued the Quraysh tribe and entered Mecca. Muhammad's sayings and practices, recorded in the Hadith and Sunnah, along with the Quran, serve as authoritative references for shaping Sharia law, which governs the lives of Muslims and their societies. Moreover, the concept of Jahiliya mentioned in the Farewell Sermon[5], delivered shortly after the conquest of Mecca and the formal establishment of Islam in Arabia, is considered by Muslims to be a significant teaching and a model for the entire religious and social system, as it was the last sermon and guidance of Muhammad's life.

After conquering Mecca, Muhammad extended gestures of reconciliation to the Quraysh tribe and other leading families of Mecca. The following year, during his pilgrimage to the Kaaba and the area around Mount Arafat, he delivered his Farewell Sermon, in which he described the previous era of blood feuds

---

[5] Albert Hourani, Translated by Kim Jung Myung & Hong Mi Jung, 『A History of the Arab Peoples』, Simsan, 2010, p.181-182.

as the spirit of Jahiliya, or the 'age of ignorance.' He declared that, with the integration of Mecca into the Muslim community and the formal emergence of Islam in Arabia, it was time to move beyond this Jahiliya.[6]

Following the authority of Muhammad's farewell sermon, contemporary Muslims and Arab historians perceive the Arabian and Arab situation before the founding of Islam as a period of Jahiliya, or ignorance. The original concept of Jahiliya primarily refers to a propensity for anger, excessive sensitivity to honor and status, arrogance, lack of restraint, and especially the chronic tendency toward violence and revenge.[7]

---

[6] "Muslims refer to this period as "Jahiliya," meaning "the Age of Ignorance." This term is contrasted with the Islamic era, which is considered the "Age of Enlightenment." Compared to the periods before or after, this era was seen as a dark age. In this sense, the advent of Islam can be seen as a kind of restoration and, as the Quran states, a restoration of the Abrahamic religions.", Bernard Lewis, 『The Middle East』, Kachibooks, 1998, p.49.

[7] Karen Amstrong, Translated by Kim Seung Wan, 『Muhammad: A Prophet for Our Time』, Gyoyangin, 2024.

Thus, the concept of Jahiliya addresses the conflicts and divisions between tribes, and the wars and clashes arising from their arrogant pride, before the Arabs universally accepted the idea of the one God, Allah. However, after Muhammad paradoxically conquered Mecca through war, he expressed the need to move beyond the animosity, wars, and Jahiliya, in order to unite with the Quraysh tribe and other groups he had fought against, using it as a term to promote post-war reconciliation and peace. Later, Muslims granted authority to this interpretation, using it as a basis for their understanding of history.

Muslims, historians, and religious leaders deeply immersed in the hyper-personality of Muhammad inevitably emphasize, whenever discussing history and eras, that the pre-Islamic history of Arabia and the Middle East was an age of ignorance. This serves as a foundation for highlighting how glorious and magnificent Islamic history truly is.[8]

For instance, let's say an Arab historian becomes interested in the small civilizations of southern Arabia before the formation of Islam and, using oral traditions and written records, describes the factors that led to the formation of these early civilizations, their languages, cultural elements, and their development. If this historian is a Muslim, when they comprehensively describe the rise, development, decline, and eventual impact of these small civilizations on Arab society, the concept of Jahiliya can function as a dogmatic authority rather than an academic one.

Under the dogmatic proclamation that Arabia was a time of ignorance before the emergence of Islam, even if a Muslim historian were to describe how the small civilizations of southern

---

[8] "Southwest Asia, North Africa, and the vast surrounding regions that would later form the Islamic world, the Caliphate's dominion, and what is today called the Arab world, were once home to different languages, religions, and rulers. Yet, within nearly a century of Muhammad's death, the entire region was transformed, undergoing one of the most rapid and dramatic changes in human history.", Bernard Lewis, the Book in front, p.59.

Arabia contributed to the formation of Arab society, including their rise and fall and their subsequent impact on Arab society, any statement about the development of these civilizations would inevitably be seen as a reaction against Muhammad's dogmatic authority that the pre-Islamic era was a time of darkness, Jahiliya.

Although the primitive small civilizations of southern Arabia undoubtedly went through periods of decline, they clearly possessed a civilized system and contributed to the formation and development of Arab society. Describing this would contradict the concept of Jahiliya. (In fact, the study of the contributions of early Arab civilizations before Islam has largely survived through the acceptance of Arab poetry, one of the traditional oral forms that Muhammad often employed.)[9]

Therefore, for a researcher who is a Muslim, mentioning and elaborating on the possibility of the development of civilizations during the pre-Islamic Jahiliya era would be in conflict

---

[9] Albert Hourani, the Book in front, p.34–38

with the authority and statements of the Islamic prophet Muhammad, particularly the concept of Jahiliya. This has placed significant constraints on the study and description of early Arab history.

Moreover, the motif of Jahiliya from Muhammad's Farewell Sermon has greatly inspired modern Islamic extremism. Sayyid Qutb, the second leader of the Muslim Brotherhood and a key modern Islamic extremist thinker, defined all history and territories not governed by Sharia law as Jahiliya.[10] He degraded Islamic systems or histories contaminated by Western materialism as having deviated from the true early Islam established by Muhammad. By labeling Islamic dynasties or regimes that were corrupted by other ideologies as being in a state of Ja-

---

10 "Jahiliya was not confined to the pre-Islamic era. We are surrounded by Jahiliyya even today… Our entire environment, including people's beliefs, thoughts, habits, art, rules, and laws, is Jahiliya. Even what we consider Islamic culture, the roots of Islam, Islamic philosophy, and Islamic thought can be seen as products of Jahiliya. We must return to the pure source from which the early Muslims learned, the most pristine source that is unmixed and uncontaminated by other things.", Sayyid Qutb, the Book in front, p.74-75

hiliya, he advocated for their rejection and elimination.

In other words, Qutb argued that any system, history, or era not governed by Sharia was a return to Jahiliya and should be rejected, eradicated, and eliminated as a reaction against Muhammad's words and deeds and the light of the founding of Islam.

For instance, extremists influenced by Qutb's ideology argue that Saudi Arabia, despite being an Islamic state, has become evil and darkness by providing military bases to the United States, thus reverting to the era of Jahiliya and should be eradicated.[11] This extreme interpretation of Jahiliya, which can negate and eliminate even established histories and regimes, has become a central motif and ideology of contemporary Islamic extremism.

---

11 "There is the pressure of the difficult circumstances imposed by the Western Christian world and the malicious attacks on jihad by evil Orientalists.", Sayyid Qutb, the Book in front, p.184
"The radical Islamic cleric, Omar Abdel-Rahman, immigrated to the United States from Egypt in 1990 and preached the teachings of Sayyid Qutb's "Milestones." He defined the United States as a nation that oppresses the world's Muslims and argued that it was a duty to fight against this "enemy of God.", 9/11Commission, 「Final Report on Terrorist Attacks Upon the Unite States(The 9/11 Commission Report)」, 2004, p.72

2) Ibn Khaldun's al-asabiyyah and the Arab tribes, the relationship between the origins of early Arab history and historical writing

- The establishment of the Islamic system through the asabiyya solidarity and the Asabiyyah of Muhammad, the Quraysh
- Asabiyyah historical view derived from the corruption of medieval Islamic dynasties

Ibn Khaldun can be positioned as a scholar who analyzed the characteristics of Arab tribes and pre-agricultural nomads prior to the establishment of religious and political systems in early Islamic Arab history. He can also be regarded as a scholar who studied the Arab prototype. However, his research, which analyzed the early nomadic forms of Arabs, including the Bedouin, was not intended to study the origins or early history of pre-Islamic Arabs. Therefore, his contribution to the study of early Arab history is limited.

First, through his Muqaddimah (Prolegomena), Ibn Khaldun introduced the concept of Asabiyyah, the collective spirit of tribal solidarity, which unites tribal factions and their purity to form political, religious, and civilizational systems. This historical perspective has had a profound influence on both Eastern and Western historians. Furthermore, he argued that dynasties and religious civilizational systems that emerged from such a spirit of solidarity, maintain a stronger cohesion than the tribes, eventually lose their original spirit of pure solidarity, they decay due to the luxury, corruption, and moral decline of the ruling dynasty, leading to their collapse. This, in turn, invites the challenge of another Asabiyyah group, creating a cyclical rise and fall of tribal dynasties and religious-civilizational systems.

This is the core of his historical view.[12]

Arnold Joseph Toynbee, Kim Hodong, and others have stated that Ibn Khaldun's unique and exceptional historical consciousness, along with his scholarly contributions, represent a singular philosophy of history, developed without being influenced by the existing paradigms of historical philosophy from medieval historians before or after his time.

While 'Muqaddimah' is merely an introduction to world history, based on Ibn Khaldun's own philosophy, incorporating independent oral interviews, bibliographic information from libraries, and bureaucratic documents, it covers a vast array of concepts and perspectives. These include Arab tribes,

---

12 In the Muqaddimah, Ibn Khaldun summarizes as follow.
"The ultimate goal of Asabiyyah is kingship / The obstacle to kingship is when the tribesmen settle into luxury and comfort / By its very nature, kingship monopolizes glory, and after indulging in luxury and a stable life, it enters a period of decline / The expansion of a dynasty's domain reaches its peak at first, then gradually diminishes, until finally the dynasty comes to an end and disappears.", Ibn Khaldun, Translated by Kim Jeong-A, 『The Muqaddimah, Records of Islamic history and civilization』, Somyungbooks, 2020, p.230-232, 277, 486.

urban dwellers, intellectuals, civilizations, dynasties, climate zones and their civilizational influences, pastoralism, agriculture, technology, commerce, profit, and accumulation. As even Toynbee acknowledged, Ibn Khaldun holds a singular position as a historian in the Islamic world.[13]

Nevertheless, despite his innate genius as a historian, it is difficult to argue that such a monumental work of historical writing could have been developed entirely independently, without any influence from paradigms or perspectives of historical interpretation, especially during the medieval period of the Maghreb Arab world, where Islamic dynasties were repeatedly declining.

---

[13] "Ibn Khaldun appears to have drawn no inspiration from any predecessors in the intellectual field he chose, found no peers among his contemporaries to match his intellect, and failed to ignite a spark of inspiration in any successors. Nevertheless, in his 『Muqaddimah』, which he appended to his world history, he conceived and shaped a unique philosophy of history—one that undoubtedly stands as the greatest work ever discussed by anyone, anywhere, at any time." (Author, quoted from Arnold Toynbee's 『A Study of History』), Kim Ho Dong, 『An Islamic classic that revealed the secrets of the rise and fall of civilization-the Muqaddimah of Ibn Khaldun』, 『Reading Oriental Classics 1 (History/Politics)』, Humanist, 2006.

In order to reconstruct the paradigms that influenced Ibn Khaldun's historical perception of Arab tribes and Asabiyyah in his Muqaddimah, it is essential to first understand the circumstances and viewpoints that likely shaped his perspective. First, during Ibn Khaldun's time, amidst the decline of Islamic dynasties in the Arab world surrounding medieval North Africa, the Maghreb still harbored Berber and Bedouin Arab tribal cultures that had not yet been assimilated into dynastic systems or urban civilizations like today's Bedouins. Second, from a young age, Ibn Khaldun had a deep devotion to Islam, memorizing the Qur'an and being strongly drawn to the purity of Muhammad and the Islamic faith.[14] Therefore, for Ibn Khaldun, Muhammad was inevitably the first model who emerged from the Quraysh tribe, utilizing group solidarity—Asabiyyah—to unite the fragmented and divided tribes through religious spirituality,

---

14 "In his(Ibn Khaldun) 『Autobiography』, it is recorded that during this period, he studied and memorized the Islamic scripture, the 『Quran』, as well as the 『Hadith』, which documents the sayings and actions of the Prophet Muhammad. He also received education in Arabic grammar, religious law, and mysticism.", Kim Ho Dong, the Book in front.

establishing Islam and laying the groundwork for the Caliphate system. However, due to his devout faith, Ibn Khaldun could not treat Muhammad as an academic subject for analysis or study. Instead, he could only approach Muhammad as a figure of dogmatic authority and as a model within the framework of Muslim religious belief. This represents a significant limitation in his academic research. For Ibn Khaldun, Muhammad represented religious authority, and his history served as an overarching paradigm. Yet, as an academic subject, Muhammad's status transcended scholarly authority, becoming an object of profound reverence and following.

In fact, considering this analogy, the most ideal model of Ibn Khaldun's Asabiyyah (group solidarity) is Muhammad, the founder of Islam. Born into the Quraysh tribe, Muhammad received revelations from Allah and, in the process of founding Islam, was rejected by the Quraysh tribe, his original community, which led him to relocate. However, he later reorganized the Arab tribes through religious spirituality, reclaimed Mecca, and unified the Quraysh tribe with a strong sense of religious solidarity. This reorganization not only unified the tribe but also gave rise to a system beyond tribal solidarity, ultimately establishing the Caliphate political system of Islam.[15]

If we reconstruct Ibn Khaldun's concept of solidarity (Asabiyyah) in light of his religious faith[16] and his perspective as a historian of the medieval era, it can be seen as an application

---

15 "Religion eliminates their arrogance and helps them suppress jealousy and envy among themselves. When a prophet or saint arises among them and commands them to follow Allah's orders, removing blameworthy traits and cultivating praiseworthy virtues, their strength becomes unified, guided towards the truth, and they attain dominion and kingship on the foundation of unity. Under proper guidance, they are the quickest to accept religious truth, as their nature has not been corrupted by depraved habits or base qualities. If they have any flaw, it is 'barbarism,' but this, too, is easily resolved once they embrace religion.", Ibn Khaldun, Translated by Kim Jeong-A, the Book in front, p.250.

16 Ibn Khaldun did not limit the concept of 'Asabiyyah' to royal authority alone, but stated that it serves as a standard in the following cases.
① Asabiyyah is not exclusive to Arab Bedouin tribes.
② Asabiyyah is absolutely necessary in missionary work.
③ Asabiyyah provides the ultimate answer to the claim that Quraysh lineage is a condition for being an Imam.
Kim Jeong-A, 「A Study on Asabiyyah in the Muqaddimah of Ibn Khaldun」, 『Journal of Middle Eastern Affairs』 Vol.16 No.4, 2017, p.35-58.

of the ideal form of solidarity he derived from Muhammad to the situation of the medieval Maghreb Islamic dynasties during Ibn Khaldun's lifetime. In other words, just as tribal solidarity was elevated through religious unity in Muhammad's case, leading to the formation of the Caliphate and dynastic systems, the same solidarity was lost in the medieval Islamic dynasties through economic accumulation and decadence. This loss of solidarity, due to luxury and corruption, ultimately led to the replacement of these dynasties by others with heightened solidarity from surrounding tribes—a reflection and lesson on the course of Islamic history. Despite being a scholar capable of utilizing oral traditions, libraries, and royal documents, the fact that Ibn Khaldun's research on Arab tribes did not extend to tracing their origins and reconstructing early Arab history represents a significant loss in terms of historical methodology, despite his vast scholarly achievements.

3) Bernard Lewis's method of describing Middle Eastern history through absence and omission of pre-Islamic Arab history

As a prominent Western scholar of Arab, Middle Eastern, and Islamic studies, Bernard Lewis' writings and perspectives have profoundly influenced the world's understanding of the Middle East and Arab-Islamic culture for nearly a century. As a British scholar, he inherited the historical narrative paradigm prevalent in mainstream Western academia that views the formation of Hellenistic, Roman, and European civilizations through the transfusion of knowledge from earlier civilizations like Akkad, Babylon, Persia, and Egypt. Lewis demonstrated vast expertise and research across the broader Middle Eastern region, including Turkey, Persia, Egypt, and Judaism.

Nevertheless, his research on ancient Arab history is relatively lacking compared to his deep expertise in other ancient Middle Eastern regions. Despite compiling works like 『The Arabs in History』 and 『The Middle East: A Brief History of the Last 2,000 Years』 during his lifetime, demonstrating his capability to discuss Arab history, which plays a significant role in the broader Middle East narrative, his treatment of ancient Arab history remains brief. In 『The Middle East: A Brief History』, for example, he provides only a few lines to trace the origins of the Arabs and pre-Islamic Arab history, despite offering a sweeping overview of the ancient Middle Eastern world.[17] Now, if we trace the origins of the Arabs, who founded Islam and had a profound impact on the Middle East, their ancient history dates back to approximately 2000 BC, starting from Abraham and Ishmael. However, much of Arab history has been predominantly framed within Islamic history after the emergence of Muhammad, which begins around AD 700. This leaves us with a mere 1,400 years of recorded history. Yet, from the life of Ishmael, the forefather of the Arabs, to the emergence of Islam, the ancient Arab history spans about 2,700 years. While the ancient history of many nations and civilizations is often summarized, there is rarely a case where the history of a key Middle Eastern people or civilization is so condensed or underrepresented. Arabs are almost unique in this regard, as their ancient history—before the rise of Islam is often mentioned only briefly, without the depth afforded to other civilizations

---

[17] Bernard Lewis, the Book in front, p.48-49

like Egypt, the Turks, Persia, Babylon, the Hebrews, Greece, or Rome. In fact, Arab history before Islam is often so minimally described that it barely qualifies as part of the broader ancient historical narrative. Instead, it is vaguely summarized as a precursor to Islamic and Middle Eastern history.

Bernard Lewis provides an overview of ancient Middle Eastern history, much like a survey of world history, tracing the civilizations of Babylon, Egypt, and Greece. He presents the ancient Middle East before the rise of Christian civilization as a bridge connecting the West and the Middle East. His approach to summarizing world ancient history and ancient Middle Eastern history shows little difference. Following this, he discusses the decline of the Byzantine Christian Empire and its conflicts with the Zoroastrian Persian Empire, highlighting the limitations and decline of these civilizations as precursors to the rise of Islamic civilization. During this period, he briefly mentions the "dark ages" of pre-Islamic Arabia before the clash and decline between the two civilizations, dedicating about two pages to it, which is nearly all that is about ancient Arab history before the advent of Islam. Even this history is briefly summarized through the Arab concept of 'Jahiliya,' or the 'Age of Ignorance,' as described by Muhammad.[18] Moreover, all of this ancient Middle Eastern history is framed from the perspective of Islam's internal viewpoint, that of a Muslim insider, portraying these events as precursors to the emergence of the 'glorious and radiant' Islamic civilization.

Bernard Lewis seems to have moved beyond the long-standing Western term "Near East" by consistently using the geopolitical concept of the "Middle East," which overcomes the Eurocentric idea of the "Near East" as merely the region close to Europe. However, while discussing the precursors and full emergence of Middle Eastern history through the lens of Islam, initiated by the Arab people, he largely omits ancient Arab history before the rise of Islam, giving it little consideration.

---

18 "The 6th century ended with both competitors in a state of decline or weakening… A series of changes had a significant impact on the Arabian Peninsula. Perhaps the most important response was that the people were no longer satisfied with their religion, the primitive idol worship they had followed until then, and began to seek a better ideology.", Bernard Lewis, the Book in front, p.50-54

Furthermore, he mainly focuses on Middle Eastern history from the 7th century onward, when the Arab-Islamic system became prominent, following its encounter with the West. This perspective is similarly reflected in the works of scholars like Albert Hourani, an Arab British historian, whose writings, such as 『A History of the Arab Peoples』, also largely bypass ancient Arab history before the advent of Islam. Like Lewis, Hourani frames Middle Eastern history as the emergence of the 'glorious Arab-Islamic civilization' following the decline of the long-standing civilizations weakened by centuries of wars and conflicts between the Western Byzantine and Persian empires.[19]

4) A study of the Arab origins of Ishmael & Islam by Hans Kung,
a former Catholic priest and scholar
- Absence of Christian evangelical perspective in Islamic studies from comparative religions perspective

---

19 Albert Hourani, the Book in front, p.25-34

Hans Küng, a former Catholic priest and a doctorate holder from the Sorbonne, is known for his work in comparative religious studies, particularly in fostering dialogue and communication with Islam. Drawing from both his Catholic background and progressive academic foundation, he has produced a comprehensive body of research that stands out in the field of Islamic studies from a Christian perspective. As a scholar of Judaism and Christianity, and with his experience as a Catholic priest, Küng holds a unique advantage in understanding these religions from an insider's perspective. He is known for writing and compiling extensive works on monotheistic religions, which could be considered a trilogy on Judaism, Christianity, and Islam.

As a result, Küng is often cited by liberal scholars and Islamic researchers alike, recognized as a prominent Christian scholar in the field of Islamic studies. Unfortunately, while Küng comes from a Catholic background and holds liberal views, there is a noticeable absence of evangelical Protestant scholars who have compiled such a comprehensive body of systematic research on Islam. Thus, Küng's work has become a representative paradigm in Christian studies on Islam.

His research on the origins of the Arabs traces the shared roots of Judaism, Christianity, and Islam through the common figure of Abraham. In doing so, Küng sheds light on the formation of the Arab people, particularly through the figure of Ishmael, the forefather of Islam. While engaging with this subject, he critiques the "clash of civilizations" theory, such as that proposed by Samuel Huntington, advocating instead for dialogue and understanding. Küng emphasizes the common ground shared by the three civilizations and traces their origins back to the Arabian Peninsula. He also highlights the significant influence of Judaism and Christianity on the development of monotheism within Islam, particularly due to the proximity of Jewish and Christian communities in the Arabian Peninsula.[20]

But Hans Küng's view draws a picture of the pre-Islamic

---

[20] Hans Küng, 『Hans Küng Islam』, Siwajinsil, 2012, p.124–125.

Arabian context as fertile ground for the common monotheistic roots of the three Abrahamic religions, with Abraham as their shared ancestor. In doing so, he ultimately argues that salvation can also exist within Islam, urging the World Council of Churches(WCC) and Catholic authorities to acknowledge the possibility of salvation outside the Church, based on a liberal and pluralistic perspective on salvation.[21]

Küng is aware of the double allegory in Galatians, where Hagar's son Ishmael is described as a child of the flesh under the law, and thus outside the promise. While he acknowledges this biblical metaphor, which suggests that Ishmael's descendants, the Arab Muslims, are outside God's promise, Küng downplays this as a limited interpretation or statement rather than the overarching intent of the Bible. He criticizes Paul's doctrine

---

21 "The reason I am raising this question so clearly is due to the particularly ambivalent attitude of the World Council of Churches… Furthermore, by doing God's will, it is the Muslims who, from the very beginning, share the most common ground with Jews and Christians… From a Christian perspective, Islam can also be a path to salvation.", Hans Küng, the Book in front, p.129-130.

in this context, arguing that this interpretation does not reflect the Bible as a whole.[22] In an effort to conclude that God's promise and salvation can also exist within Islam, Küng skillfully extracts the commonalities between Christianity and Islam as religions rooted in Abraham, using this approach to support his academic argument.[23]

However, from the perspective of evangelical Protestantism, Hans Küng's view, which discusses the origins of Islam and the possibility of salvation as a common Abrahamic religion, is entirely unacceptable. Yet, externally, this perspective tends to be positioned as the mainstream academic stance of

---

[22] "But in the Hebrew Bible, isn't Abraham's son, the son of the desert, Ishmael, thoroughly ignored when compared to Isaac? Isn't the same true in the New Testament? Isn't the Sarah–Hagar allegory in the Apostle Paul's letter to the Galatians a complete disdain for Ishmael? It's hard to directly refute such a challenge. However, that is only one aspect of the story.", Hans Küng, the Book in front, p.116.

[23] "While Abraham initially appears to be a "common denominator" among the three religions, a closer examination "from the perspective of each religion's tradition" reveals him to be, paradoxically, the "embodiment of everything that divides the three religions." Does this make it impossible to use Abraham as an "ideal starting point" for dialogue today?", Hans Küng, the Book in front, p.117–119, 123.

Christianity toward Islam. Due to Hans Küng's monumental achievement in synthesizing Islamic studies as a comparative religion and his strong academic presence, his liberal interpretation—unacceptable from a Protestant missiological or evangelical perspective—can be mistaken as the mainstream position of Christianity in academic circles. Unfortunately, while it is acknowledged that the origins of the Arab people were formed through the birth of Abraham's first son, Ishmael, if the study of Arab origins, pre-Islamic ancient history, and Islam had been organized and established from the evangelical Christian missionary perspective, Hans Küng's view would not have gained such one-sided dominance in mainstream Christian scholarship. There is an urgent need for comprehensive and outstanding research from an evangelical perspective, synthesizing the views of Protestant missiologists and missionaries to the Arab Islam world regarding the origins and history of the Arab people.

3. Beyond the Limitations of Research
-The Absence of Records on Arab Nomadic Culture and the Utilization of Islamic Intellectual Archives Influenced by Hellenistic Thought

From the perspective of authorities who have shaped the paradigm of Arab historical viewpoints, there is a significant oversight regarding the origins of the Arabs, both in the West and within the Middle East. Additionally, prior to the systematization of Islam as a religion, Arabs lived as nomads, and their sedentary written record culture was weak.[24] Consequently, the lack of records on pre-Islamic Arabs presents a disadvantage in studying Arab origins and the history preceding Islam. However, Islam, having borrowed narratives from the Old and New

---

24 Jeon Wan Gyung, the Book in front, p.18~20.
Hans Küng, the Book in front, p.80-84.

Testaments, contains significant internal contradictions within the Qur'an, making it incomparable to the internal consistency and unity of the Bible. To compensate for these contradictions, Islam sought to mediate and justify them through the use of Hellenistic intellectualism. Ironically, this opened the door for the infusion of Hellenistic thought into Islamic society, leading to intellectual accumulation by establishing various libraries and academies in the Arab Mediterranean region.[25] Therefore, by utilizing the relatively accurate oral tradition of Arab culture and the intellectual archives that have systematically remained within Arab society after its encounter with Hellenistic thought, it would be beneficial for scholars, theorists, and even missionaries to challenge themselves to academic systematization and open a new scholarly paradigm regarding the origins of the Arabs, an introduction to their history, and the pre-Islamic era. Such field researchers could pioneer new approaches to studying and understanding Arab history through these resources. The study of Arab origins and pre-Islamic history is crucial

---

[25] Encyclopedia Britannica Editors, 『The Britannica Guide to the Islamic World』, Agora, 2017, p.74~85

for gaining a deep understanding of the Middle East, offering powerful insights into the region's identity. However, due to the reasons mentioned earlier, this area remains largely untouched, resembling uncharted academic territory. While extensive scholarly research on the Middle Eastern Arabs has spanned from ancient and medieval times to the modern era, this specific domain remains a field ripe for pioneering study. Should research achievements in this area be substantiated, it could open new academic paradigms and frameworks, marking a significant advancement in the field.

4. The Origins of Arabs in the Bible
– The Genealogy of Arabs Traced through Ishmael and Muhammad

Interestingly, while Arabs identify the southern Arabs centered around Saudi Arabia as "Qahtan," they do not consider them to be the direct lineal or spiritual descendants of Ishmael and Muhammad. Instead, they refer to the northern Arabs as

"Adnan," viewing them as the direct lineal and spiritual heirs of Ishmael and Muhammad.[26] It is evident from the Old Testament that Ishmael and Hagar, who were of Egyptian origin, were expelled from Abraham's household, lost their way at the borders of Egypt, and then migrated southward into Arabia.[27] But why do Arabs consider the northern Arabs to be the direct lineal descendants of Ishmael and Muhammad? Generally, Arabs have maintained a clear record of their genealogical lines to the extent that names are often marked by family and paternal lineage. Ultimately, the root cause can be traced back to the Bible, where the answer is found in the marriage between Ishmael's family and Esau. According to the Bible, the origins and identity of the northern Arabs are revealed when Ishmael's

---

26 Jeon Wan Gyung, the Book in front, p.22~25.

27 While he was living in the Desert of Paran, his mother got a wife for him from Egypt(Genesis 21:21)

daughter is recorded as marrying Esau.(Genesis 25:13, 28:9)[28] Additionally, Ishmael's second son Kedar and his descendants, who settled in the northern region, are mentioned along with Arabia.(Isaiah 60:6-7, Ezekiel 27:20-22)[29]

Thus, the northern Arabs were formed through this lineage and can be found today in regions such as Jordan, Lebanon, Syria, and Palestine. It was among these northern Arabs that Muhammad, the founder of Islam, emerged. Therefore, the ge-

---

[28] These are the names of the sons of Ishmael, listed in the order of their birth: Nebaioth the firstborn of Ishmael, Kedar, Adbeel, Mibsam.(Genesis 25:13)
so he went to Ishmael and married Mahalath, the sister of Nebaioth and daughter of Ishmael son of Abraham, in addition to the wives he already had.(Genesis 28:9)

[29] Herds of camels will cover your land, young camels of Midian and Ephah. And all from Sheba will come, bearing gold and incense and proclaiming the praise of the LORD. All Kedar's flocks will be gathered to you, the rams of Nebaioth will serve you; they will be accepted as offerings on my altar, and I will adorn my glorious temple.(Isaiah 60:6–7)
Dedan traded in saddle blankets with you. Arabia and all the princes of Kedar were your customers; they did business with you in lambs, rams and goats. The merchants of Sheba and Raamah traded with you; for your merchandise they exchanged the finest of all kinds of spices and precious stones, and gold.(Ezekiel 27:20–22)

nealogical line linking Ishmael to Muhammad is recognized by today's Arab society as being rooted not in the southern Arabs of Saudi Arabia, but in the northern Arabs.

Furthermore, when understanding Arab society, it is essential to recognize that, despite the profound influence of the Islamic system on the Arab world, the fundamental structure of the Arab people remains that of family-based tribes, as recorded in the Bible. Arab society was historically divided and formed by distinct tribes, each with its own identity. To grasp the intrinsic spirit and internal order of the Arabs, one must first comprehend the ancient tribalism that forms the basis of Arab culture.

5. Research on Arab origins and Reevaluation of the Study Scope in Introductory of Arab Studies, Middle Eastern Studies, and Islamic Studies
– Including North Africa region, Central Asia region, and Southeast Asia region

Given that the origin of the Arabs is based on the Bible, with the lineage of northern Arabs developing through the marriage between Ishmael's daughter and Esau, and other sons such as Kedar's lineage, forming a broader northern Arab group that leads to the lineage of Muhammad, it is possible to trace the genealogical origins of Arabs and the founder of Islam. When distinguishing between this genealogical Arab origin and the emergence of Islam, it becomes clear that there is a need to reestablish the framework of academic research in Arab and Islamic studies to include regions influenced by Arab-Islamic culture, such as the Middle East, North Africa, Central Asia, and Southeast Asia. Yet, the boundaries of academic research have often been ambiguous: are they defined by genealogical ties, linguistic compatibility, Islamic religious heritage, or geopolitical location?

The concept of the "Middle East" itself emerged in reaction to the Western-centric term "Near East." Thus, despite being the core region where Arab culture and Islam originated, the term "Middle East" is a vague geopolitical concept that does not fully encapsulate the characteristics of Arab Islam.[30]

Ethnically and genealogically, as previously mentioned, Arabs are divided into northern and southern groups, with the direct lineage tracing back to Ishmael and Muhammad concentrated among the northern Arabs. Meanwhile, Islam, which arose in Mecca and Medina in southern Arabia, continues to have its religious center of gravity in Saudi Arabia. Thus, the

---

30 Nam Sik In(Professor in Korea National Diplomatic Academy), 2022.
https://www.youtube.com/watch?v=FHcm7B_VjVE

heart of the Arab world from a religious perspective is rooted in southern Arabia after the 7th century.[31]

So, what criteria are used to distinguish the research scope for North Africa, Central Asia, and Southeast Asia's Islamic regions? Are these regions categorized based on geopolitical concepts like the "Middle East"? Are they grouped by genealogical or ethnic Arab identity, or by the religious spirit of Islam? The boundaries remain unclear. In the case of North Africa, despite being loosely grouped under the umbrella of "Arab" due to the influence of Islam, it is never referred to in academic or general terms as "Central Asian Arabs," even though Central Asia was also significantly impacted by Islam. If so, does it mean the North African region is Arab in terms of bloodline and ethnicity just because it was influenced by Islam? Why is the term 'Arab' used for North Africa when there is almost no bloodline connection to North African people, as there is for Southern and Northern Arabs? It seems that 'Arab' in North Africa is a

---

31 Jeon Wan Gyung, the Book in front, p.33–34.

concept distinguished by linguistic commonality. In contrast to Central Asia, which was also Islamized, the current North African region continues to use and employ Modern Standard Arabic as its public language.[32] Therefore, the term "Arab" in the context of the "Arab" world of North Africa is not a distinction based on bloodline, tribe, ethnicity, or religious identity but rather a distinction based on the shared language of Modern Standard Arabic.

In contrast, in Central Asia and Southeast Asia, despite the spread of the Quran in Arabic, these regions did not adopt Arabic as their everyday language, unlike North Africa. Hence, terms like "Central Asian Arabs" or "Southeast Asian Arabs" are not used in the same way.

In conclusion, the study of the Middle East, Arabs, Islam, and the Arab identity in North Africa, Central Asia, and South-

---

[32] "A university professor in Morocco argues that "Arabism is essentially language and culture.", Jeon Wan Gyung, the Book in front, p.36.

east Asia requires a more precise and consistent set of academic research boundaries and classification criteria. It is rare for a field of study to have such a mixed scope of academic research, combining geopolitical, linguistic, genealogical/ethnic, and religious concepts without established criteria for academic consensus. It seems that the origin of the Arabs as derived from the Bible has been overlooked or inadequately addressed, and the history has been predominantly narrated through the lens of post-7th century Islamic expansion and interactions with Western geopolitical developments. It gives the impression that the first paragraph is vaguely inserted.

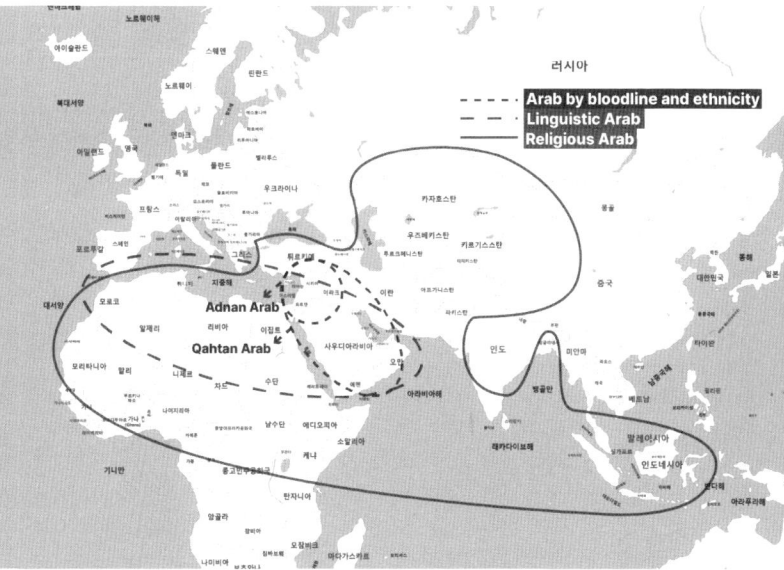

6. Understanding the Foundations of Pre-Islamic Arab Society and Arab Tribalism: Modern Application Cases
 - The Israel-Hamas War and Peace Solutions

Recently, federalism has been newly proposed, primarily in Western circles, in the context of the Israel-Hamas war. The international community had previously suggested solutions such as the two-state solution[33] for Israel and Palestine , as well as the one-state, one-system[34] approach centered around Israel. However, these approaches have proven difficult to realize.

---

[33] Two-state solution, The establishment of a Jewish state of Israel and a Palestinian state for the Palestinian people as a solution to the Israeli-Palestinian conflict was part of the Oslo Accords of 1993. Britannica, https://www.britannica.com/topic/two-state-solution

[34] One state solution, Yousef Munayyer (Secretary-General of the Jerusalem Fund for Palestinian Center) argued for 'the establishment of a constitution that guarantees equal rights for Palestinians, overcoming the past through truth-seeking and reparations, and establishing a single state.', Foreign Affairs, 2019.

Thus, a new proposal has emerged: forming a loose federal state, similar to the United States, that recognizes the autonomy of both Israel and Palestine. The perspective presented, appeals to the international community by using the analogy that a one-state theory is like a complete marriage, a two-state theory is akin to a divorce, and a federal-state theory[35], is similar to consensual cohabitation, fundamentally borrowing motifs from a Western framework. However, this viewpoint lacks an understanding of the roots and particularities of the Middle East and Arab societies and attempts to interpret this extreme conflict through a lens of self-serving convenience.

This is because the ancient conflict[36] between Ishmael and Isaac, which shaped the roots of the Middle Eastern Arab-Israeli conflict, is fundamentally based on the tribal vendettas and

---

35 The Kedar Plan (Eight—State Solution) proposes a UAE—style federation of seven major tribes in the West Bank, with international support for its establishment, Nam Sik In, 2018.

36 But Sarah saw that the son whom Hagar the Egyptian had borne to Abraham was mocking, and she said to Abraham, "Get rid of that slave woman and her son, for that slave woman's son will never share in the inheritance with my son Isaac. (Genesis 21:9—10)

blood feuds of the Middle East. These feuds are rooted in the ancient Middle Eastern law of "an eye for an eye, a tooth for a tooth," and this tradition has been passed down through generations, continuing to influence the dynamics within the region. This stems from traditions rooted in the Middle Eastern Arab culture before the formalization of Islam, and even Muhammad could not overcome this prototype of Arab tribalism. Although Muhammad referred to the pre-Islamic period of tribal conflict and social division as "Jahiliya" (the age of ignorance), he himself could not fully escape the entrenched vendettas and hostilities inherent in Arab tribalism. Despite unifying tribalism under the belief in monotheism, the deep-seated grievances among the Arab tribes persisted. When Muhammad migrated from Mecca to Medina, he faced opposition from the Arab Jewish tribes who disregarded his claim as a prophet. In retaliation, driven by this hostile relationship, Muhammad carried out brutal massacres against them, enslaving their women and children. This cycle of vengeance ultimately led to his death, as he was poisoned by those harboring deep-seated resentment against him. Thus, his life ended amidst the very same conflicts and tribal vendettas that had shaped much of the pre-Islamic Middle Eastern society.

Therefore, the legal and cultural tradition of "an eye for an eye, a tooth for a tooth" in the Middle East forms the foundation for understanding Arab societies today. The extreme conflict between Israel and Hamas, as well as the broader tensions involving Palestine and Arab Islamic societies, are often interpreted naively through a simplistic Western lens that focuses solely on systemic structures. This is because the deep-rooted historical and cultural foundations of the Arab world are overlooked. The relationships of enmity and vengeance in Arab tribalism take precedence over systems, governments, or religion, and are more fundamental in shaping societal dynamics. Therefore, the war between Israel and Hamas only intensifies the resentment based on tribalism, and cannot be resolved through governance structures, systems, or interventions by international organizations. Peace can only be achieved through the gospel of forgiveness and the message of reconciliation, which surpasses and fulfills the demands of the law.

References

- Kim Jeong-A, 「A Study on Asabiyyah in the Muqaddimah of Ibn Khaldun」, 「Journal of Middle Eastern Affairs」 Vol.16 No.4, p.35-58, 2017.
- Kim Ho Dong, 「An Islamic classic that revealed the secrets of the rise and fall of civilization-the Muqaddimah of Ibn Khaldun」, 「Reading Oriental Classics 1 (History/Politics)」, Humanist, 2006.
- Bernard Lewis, 「The Arabs in History」, Oxford University Press(1993)
- Encyclopedia Britannica Editors, 「The Britannica Guide to the Islamic World」, Encyclopedia Britannica, Inc., 2009
- Sayyid Qutb, 「Milesstone」, Islamic Book Service, 2006
- Song Kyung-Keun, 「A Study on the Asabiyah of Ibn Khaldun」, 「Collection of writings of Korean Association Of The Middle East Studies」 Book No.36, Ch.3
- Albert Hourani, 「A History of the Arab Peoples」, Grand Central Pub(1992)
- Ibn Khaldun, Translated by Kim Jeong-A, 「The Muqaddimah, Records of Islamic history and civilization」, Somyungbooks, 2020.
- Ibn Khaldun, Translated by Kim Ho Dong, 「The Muqaddimah - Arab, Islam, Civilization」, Kachibooks, 2003.
- Jeon Wan Gyung, 「Arab Cultural History」, Korean Studies Information, 2013
- Karen Amstrong, 「Muhammad: A Prophet for Our Time」, HarperOne, 2007.
- Hans Küng, 「Hans Küng Islam」, Oneworld Publications, 2007
- 9/11 Commission, 「Final Report on Terrorist Attacks Upon the Unite States(The 9/11 Commission Report)」, 2004

Research tasks on the Origins of the Remaining Arab Peoples